THE

MAGDEBURG

CONFESSION

13th of April 1550 AD

TRANSLATED BY
MATTHEW COLVIN

INTRODUCTION BY
GEORGE GRANT

ISBN: 1470087537
ISBN 13: 9781470087531

Library of Congress Control Number: 2012903108
CreateSpace, North Charleston, SC

ON THE COVER

Woodcut of a bearwolf, by Hans Weiditz, 1517 AD.

The bearwolf was a monster of German folklore. Martin Luther used the bearwolf as a symbol of tyranny. The pastors of Magdeburg wrote of it in the *Magdeburg Confession* while speaking of the fourth and most severe level of tyranny.

A soldier's song from that era also spoke of the bearwolf:

Give unto Caesar what is Caesar's, just as we read;
But how much more so for the Lord God!
As long as he does the Lord's will, and lives in peace,
Caesar's office we must honour;
Should he transgress, he is no more
Emperor or lord, but an outlaw
And a bearwolf against which we must guard.
[Magdeburg, 1548 AD]

TABLE OF CONTENTS

FOREWORD

How the Confession was obtained and
a brief description of the contents

I first discovered the *Magdeburg Confession* while researching to write a book on a little known tool to restrain tyranny called the *Lesser Magistrate Doctrine.* The doctrine can be traced back many centuries and supplies biblical principles by which men may justly override those in positions of higher authority to quell an abuse of power. I had read references to the *Magdeburg Confession* in my studies and, therefore, wanted to read it in its entirety. Thus began a journey to obtain a complete copy of the *Confession* in English.

After eight months of countless phone calls and emails with historians, scholars, professors, and librarians both in America and Europe, the conclusion of the matter was that an English translation simply did not exist.

Still desiring to obtain a complete copy of the *Magdeburg Confession* so that my research might be as complete as possible, I then made a simple 30-second appeal to a television audience in the Milwaukee, Wisconsin area where I host a weekly show. I asked if anyone knew how to obtain a copy of the *Confession* in English, and if so, would they please contact me.

Later that same night, when the show was being re-run, a librarian from *Concordia University,* Christian Himsel, got up to bottle-feed his infant daughter. Christian turned on the television and a minute later saw my appeal about the *Confession.* He contacted me the next day and offered to hunt the document down. I was gratified by his eagerness to assist in locating a complete copy.

After a month, however, Christian Himsel realized that indeed no English translation existed. Though the *Confession* had been translated into the common language of Magdeburg – German – it had *never* been translated into English. He therefore began to pursue locating an original which was written in Latin. All important theological works published at the time the *Magdeburg Confession* was penned were written in Latin or translated into Latin, as it was the language of commerce and scholarship in the old world.

Himsel was finally able to secure a 1550 A.D. Latin original from the *Bavarian State Library* about three months after he first offered his expertise in researching rare documents. But neither Himsel nor I were qualified to read, understand and translate the document we had acquired. Through God's providential hand, I rather quickly obtained the services of Dr. Matthew Colvin for the translation work. Dr. Colvin is eminently qualified, having earned his Ph.D. in both Latin and Greek Literature from Cornell University.

It is with this confluence of characters, skills and events that we are proudly able to present the *Magdeburg Confession* at last to an English audience. The document should be considered a valuable resource not only for theologians and Church historians, but also for those engaged in all levels of government, local and national, including civil services, law enforcement, the military and the judiciary. The *Magdeburg Confession* was written and signed by actors in an amazing drama that called into question how righteous men ought to respond to those in power and authority when such men make unjust or immoral laws or decrees.

The *Magdeburg Confession* is an important historical work because the men of Magdeburg were the first in the history of mankind to set forth in a doctrinal format what only later came to be known as the doctrine of the lesser magistrate. The pastors of Magdeburg wrote and signed the *Confession* just prior to the city entering a 13-month military siege by Emperor Charles V.

The *Lesser Magistrate Doctrine* declares that when the higher or superior authority makes an unjust or immoral law or decree, the lower or lesser magistrate has both a right and duty to refuse obedience to the superior authority. If need be, the lesser authorities even have the right and obligation to actively resist and oppose the superior authority.

Martin Luther was rescued from death by the interposition of a lesser magistrate who defied the order of his superior. Prince Frederick the Wise was Elector of Saxony, and as such, he was a lesser magistrate. His superior, Emperor Charles V, in conjunction with Pope Leo X, had ordered Luther to attend an ecclesiastical convention in Worms, Germany in the spring of 1521. Through Frederick's efforts, Luther was guaranteed safe-conduct so that he could personally answer charges and renounce or reaffirm his theological views. The reformer therefore attended the Diet.

When Luther failed to renounce his beliefs and submit to the Roman Catholic Church, Emperor Charles V ordered Luther's "apprehension." Charles forbade *"anyone from this time forward to dare, either by words or by deeds, to receive, defend, sustain, or favor the said Martin Luther"* and commanded that the reformer be brought before his court for punishment as a *"notorious heretic."* Such language was tantamount to a death sentence.

Though directly under Charles' authority, Prince Frederick did not arrest Luther and turn him over to Charles as ordered. Instead, he feigned Luther's abduction in order to hide and protect him. He used his lesser authority to contravene Charles' unjust order and defend Luther, who resided in his jurisdiction, from death.

Thirty years later, the protection afforded Luther by a lesser magistrate clearly impacted the men of Magdeburg. Emperor Charles V imposed his *Augsburg Interim* on May, 15, 1548. This law was an attempt to force Protestants back under traditional Roman Catholic beliefs, practices and rule. The men of Magdeburg refused to submit to Charles and the Roman Catholic Church. Their consciences were resolute because of their fealty to Christ, and they stood their ground because they understood the doctrine of the lesser magistrate.

The men of Magdeburg were the first in history to identify many examples of the lesser magistrate doctrine in action, both from the Bible and from human history. That they knew they had stumbled upon something new (because of their circumstances) is apparent in the *Confession* itself. They write:

We would have desired even now to hide this true opinion as it had always been hidden hitherto, had we not been defeated by the present injustice and tyranny of certain men, and deemed that the preservation of the Gospel and the True Church ought to be put before such dangers from those ignorant men.

(The "*true opinion*" that had "*always been hidden hitherto*" is the lesser magistrate doctrine.) Though the lesser magistrate doctrine was practiced long before Christianity, and though Christian men practiced this doctrine at various times in Christian history, these pastors were the first to write down the doctrine as proven sound in Scripture and practiced in history.

The first name signed to the *Magdeburg Confession* is Nicholas von Amsdorff. He was a close friend of Martin Luther, and accompanied him to his hearing at Worms in 1521. He was also with Luther on the return trip when Prince Frederick "abducted" Luther (of which Amsdorff was privy) in order to hide and protect him. Amsdorff remained a close friend until Luther's death in 1546.

The *Magdeburg Confession* consists of three parts. The first part is designed to assure the lesser magistrates of their day of the confessors' orthodoxy – that they stood four-square with Luther. Therefore, they lay out in detail their Lutheran theology. The third part is a warning and exhortation to all those who would take actions against them, whether directly or through complicity, as well as those who would stand by and do nothing to help them. This part sets forth much wisdom.

The second part of the *Confession* however, lays out the lesser magistrate doctrine. This section begins with an appeal to Charles V. The pastors exhort him to remove those he has surrounded himself with who are giving him bad counsel. They make clear to Charles that the *only* reason for this impasse is due to his attack upon their Christian faith; that when those in civil authority make law which impugns the Law or Word of God, Christian men have a duty to obey God, rather than men.

They also assure Charles that they are his best citizens. They write:

> We will give from our Churches the greatest possible number of men who, if they be able to enjoy their own religion through you, will declare their obedience toward you in all owed and upright duties, and loyalty without hypocrisy... perhaps more than all those whom you say are obedient to you.

They declare they have taken their stand against him only because of their love for Christ – and His Law and Word. Therefore their stand is sure, and they tell Charles, "*We are not swayed by the majesty or wealth of anyone.*" They then inform him that they will make plain to him "*this doctrine which we hand down about the legitimate defense of the lower magistrate against a superior.*"

In their arguments, the pastors declare the idea of unlimited obeisance to the State as "*an invention of the devil.*" They rightly assert that all authority is delegated from God. Therefore, if the one in authority makes commands contrary to the Law or Word of God, those subject to his authority have both a right not to obey, and a duty to actively resist. The pastors proffer an example from family government. They write:

> Let us take an example concerning a father of a family. If he should come to his wife or grown daughters in his house with some scoundrels in an obvious attempt to prostitute them, then his wife and daughters not only would not render their husband and father the obedience they otherwise owe him, but when they are not able to preserve their chastity in any other way, they would drive him off with stones.

The pastors then take this example and make an analogy to civil government. Their point is that no one in authority – whether in family, church, or civil government – holds his authority autonomously. Rather it is delegated to them from God. If the authority therefore makes law which contravenes the Law of God, those subject to their authority can refuse obedience because, as the pastors state, "*divine laws necessarily trump human ones.*"

To the pastors of Magdeburg, all magistrates possess delegated authority from God. Therefore, the lesser magistrates have lawful authority to oppose the superior magistrate-turned-tyrant when he makes laws contrary to the Law and Word of God.

The pastors did not view unjust or immoral law and edicts by the higher magistrate to be an *excuse* for lesser magistrates *not* to protect the citizens of their jurisdiction. Rather they viewed resistance to unjust or immoral laws and edicts by the higher magistrate as the *duty* of the lesser magistrates *to protect* the citizens of their jurisdiction.

The pastors are so detailed in their *Confession* that they carefully define four *levels* or *degrees* of tyranny by a superior magistrate, and the legitimate and proper response of the lesser magistrates to each. There was order to their resistance. Their position was well thought-out, adhered to standards, and appealed to immutable truth.

These Lutherans were *first* to set forth a doctrine on the lesser magistrate. Their writings clearly impacted other of the Reformers in Europe, including John Knox, Theodore Beza, Philipp Mornay, and Thomas Goodman – all four of whom went on to further the doctrine of the lesser magistrate.

John Knox was influenced by the *Magdeburg Confession*. During a debate in 1564 AD with William Maitland of Lethington, who was Secretary of State for Mary, Queen of Scots, Maitland chided Knox for his position that lesser magistrates and the people could oppose the higher authority stating of Knox's position, "*I think ye shall not have many learned men of your opinion.*"

Knox replied:

> My lord, the truth ceases not to be the truth, howsoever it be that men either misknow it, or yet gainstand it. And yet, I praise my God, I lack not the consent of God's servants in that head.

Knox then handed a copy of the *Magdeburg Confession* to the Secretary and bid him to read the names of the pastors signed at the end of the document declaring the just defence of the city, and then added, "*To resist a tyrant, is not to resist God, nor yet His ordinance.*"

After looking at the names of the pastors, Lethington mockingly stated, "*Men of no note.*" Upon which Knox replied of the Magdeburgers, "*Yet servants of God.*"

John Calvin's successor, Theodore Beza, when writing of the right and duty of lesser magistrates to resist superior authority which makes unjust laws or orders, said of Magdeburg, "*The city of Magdeburg, situated on the Elbe, offered the outstanding example of this in our own time.*"

Twenty years later, while writing *On the Right of Magistrates* in 1574 AD, Beza included in the title itself "*A Treatise Published by Those in Magdeburg in 1550.*" Beza first published his work anonymously due to the political situation at the time, and he thought so highly of and was so deeply influenced by the Magdeburgers, that he ascribed his writing to them.

The *Magdeburg Confession* is of vast historical significance precisely because it laid out the lesser magistrate doctrine from Holy Scripture and history.

I want to thank several people without whom this project to get *The Magdeburg Confession* into the vernacular of English-speaking people - 462 years after its composition in Latin - would not have been possible. Christian Himsel who took the task to find an original in Latin, and who I found great joy in conversing with about the things of the Lord. Matt Colvin, whose love for the Lord and for what was birthed at Magdeburg has afforded us with such an excellent and faithful translation to the original text. And George Grant, who has provided an introduction to this *Confession* which should move any man who loves Christ and Western Civilization to tears.

I would also like to thank my wife Clara, a woman who cherishes liberty and has always provoked me unto love and good works. And my eleven children, all of whom Clara birthed, who have helped me realize and remember why being vigilant of our liberties is so important.

Finally, I would like to thank the men of Magdeburg who were not only men of word, *but of deed*. They persevered for over 13 months while Charles laid seige to their city and cost 468 of them their lives in battle. May we rally to their example when we see tyranny raise its' ugly head. May we rally and support those lesser magistrates that take a stand, as the Lord has made clear in His Word is right and proper to do!

Pastor Matt Trewhella
St. Crispin's Day
Milwaukee, Wisconsin

INTRODUCTION

By George Grant

One of the most distinctive features of the Biblical worldview is the principle of covenant or federalism. In Christian theological parlance, the covenant is the personal, binding, structural relationship among the Persons of the triune Godhead and His people. This sort of federalism is thus the sovereignly initiated divine-to-human, human-to-divine, and human-to-human social structure. Essentially what that means is that the covenant becomes the means by which we approach, deal with, and know God – as well as one another. It is the pattern of our relationship and our relationships, our community and our communities. In a very real sense it is the "unified field theory" of Biblical theology.

As opposed to the myriad of non-Christian contract-initiated or compact-based social relationships which are invariably impersonal, structural, and ideological (whether they be tribal, linguistic, or political), a covenantal or federal society is organic and relational, personal and familial, neither wholly individual or exclusively corporatistic.

A comprehensive covenantal or federal view reinforces the notion that every life is sacred, that no person is expendable, that everyone in a society is responsible to someone and for someone. And the practical outworking of such a profound caveat to the normal state of human affairs in this poor fallen world is more than a little astonishing.

A covenantal social structure, for instance, produces spheres of sovereignty where divisions of responsibility, authority, and labor – reinforced with suitable checks and balances – are put into place. Thus, federalism produces a separation of powers by means of the rule of law rather than the imposition of arbitrary justice from ideological or impersonal forces. It also provides for such essential principles of freedom as magistratal interpositionalism as well as popular representation and the consent of the governed.

All this, from this great innovation among men and nations: the idea of a federal covenant.

Indeed, this was the essential philosophical and structural framework within which the American Founding Fathers constructed their innovative scheme of national checks and balances, separation of powers, and mixed government. The covenantal development of state confederation, or federalism, allowed for distinctive and individual communities to join together for a greater good without losing their essential distinctiveness and individuality. Instead of the states becoming a part of some larger amorphous union, under federalism they were able to unite in a symbiotic fashion so that the sum of their parts might be greater than that of the whole.

As the American Patriots imagined it, a federal relationship would be a kind of confession of first principles or covenant that would allow states to bind themselves together substantially without entirely subsuming their sundry identities. The federal nature of the American Constitutional covenant would enable the nation to function as a republic – thus specifically avoiding the dangers of a pure democracy. Republics exercise governmental authority through mediating representatives under the rule of law. Pure democracies on the other hand exercise governmental authority through the imposition of the will of the majority without regard for the concerns of any minority – thus allowing law to be subject to the whims, fashions, and fancies of men. The Founders designed federal system of the United States so that the nation could be, as John Adams described it, a "government of law, not of men."

The Founders thus expressly and explicitly rejected the idea of a pure democracy, just as surely as totalitarian monarchy, because as James Madison declared "democracies have ever been spectacles of turbulence and contention; have ever been found incompatible with personal security, or the rights of property; and have in general been as short in their lives, as they have been violent in their deaths." The rule of the majority does not always respect the rule of law, and is as turbulent as the caprices of political correctness or dictatorial autonomy.) Indeed, history has proven all too often that democracy is particularly susceptible to the urges and impulses of mobocracy.

Federalism balances the vertical and horizontal aspects of a covenant. Vertically, Americans are one people under the rule of common law. Horizontally though, Americans are differentiated into a number of distinctive communities – sovereign states – protected from the possible intrusions of the national government or from a majority of the other communities. As educator Paul Jehle has argued, "The nature of federalism is seen in the balanced structure of the states and the people throughout the Constitution. Both the national government and State governments are sovereign in their respective spheres. Our national identity as Americans, and our federal identity as state citizens, are both represented in Congress – in the Senate and House."

Even such constitutional provisions as the Electoral College were originally designed by the Founders as a covenantal hedge against the domination of the absolute national majority over the individual states – indeed, without the College, the delicate federal balance between national unity and regional distinctiveness would be lost and the various states would lose much of their power over the executive branch.

Alas, the essential principles of covenantalism or federalism have only rarely been practiced. Early America was very much the exception.

In ancient Israel, we see the fruits of covenantalism only sporadically. But, when they prevailed, the results were an extraordinary influence and prosperity all out of proportion to Israel's size and power. Likewise, the slow emergence of Christendom during the waning years of the Roman hegemony produced a flowering of art, music, literature, economic progress, and technological development the likes of which the world had never before seen.

But, the greatest leap forward in the development of covenantalism or federalism came during the Medieval Age. This remarkable period has commonly been called the Dark Ages – as if the light of civilization had been unceremoniously snuffed out. It has similarly been dubbed the Middle Ages – as if it were a gaping parenthesis in mankind's long upward march to modernity. It was in fact, anything but dark or middling. Perhaps our greatest fault in the modern world is that we have limited ourselves by parochialism in time. It is difficult for us to attribute anything but backwardness to those epochs and cultures that do not share our peculiar goals or aspirations.

The Medieval period was actually quite remarkable for its many advances – perhaps unparalleled in all of history. It was a true nascence, while the epoch that followed was but a re-naissance. It was a new and living thing that gave flower to a culture marked by energy and creativity. From the monolithic security of Byzantium in the East to the reckless diversity of feuding fiefs in the West it was a glorious crazy quilt of human fabrics, textures, and hues.

Now to be sure, the medieval world was racked with abject poverty, ravaging plagues, and petty wars – much like our own day. It was haunted by superstition, prejudice, and corruption – as is the modern era. And it was beset by consuming ambition, perverse sin, and damnable folly – again, so like today. Still, it was free from the kind of crippling sophistication, insular ethnocentricity, and cosmopolitan provincialism that now shackles us – and so it was able to advance astonishingly.

The titanic innovations Medievalism brought forth were legion: it gave birth to all the great universities of the world from Oxford and Cambridge to Leipzig to Mainz; it oversaw the establishment of all the great hospitals of the world from St. Bartholomew's and Bedlam in London to St. Bernard's and Voixanne in Switzerland; it brought forth the world's most celebrated artists from Michelangelo Buonarotti and Albrecht Durer to Leonardo da Vinci and Jan van Eyck; it gave us the splendor of Gothic architecture – unmatched and unmatchable to this day – from Notre Dame and Chartres to Winchester and Cologne; it thrust out into howling wilderness and storm tossed seas the most accomplished explorers from Amerigo Vespucci and Marco Polo to Vasco da Gama and Christopher Columbus; it produced some of the greatest minds and most fascinating lives mankind has yet known – were the list not so sterling it might begin to be tedious – Copernicus, Dante, Giotto, Becket, Gutenberg, Chaucer, Charlemagne, Wyclif, Magellan, Botticelli, Donatello, Petrarch, and Aquinas.

But of all the great innovations that medievalism wrought, the greatest of all was the application of covenantal federalism to the whole of society and life in a system called feudalism.

In 476 the fierce Heruli military commander, Odoacer, deposed the last Western emperor, Romulus Augustulus. Though historians make much of that date – supposing it to mark the ignominious end of the Roman imperial era – in reality, no one then supposed that the empire ceased to exist. For centuries past, even though it was governed by two competing emperors – one in the East at Constantinople and one in the West at Rome or Ravenna – the empire continued to be regarded as a single whole. So, when Romulus was forced into exile, Odoacer and the other barbarian leaders did not hesitate to recognize the formal and universal overlordship of the Eastern emperor, Zeno.

Though the Ostrogoths, Vandals, Franks, Visigoths, Lombards, and Burgundians all set up new kingdoms in the Western provinces, they never questioned the abiding significance of the confederated empire. Kingship merely denoted leadership of a clan or a community: such leaders continued to look to the emperor to grant them titles to both land and authority. They used the emperor's image on their coins. They adopted Roman law throughout the provinces. And they paid fealty to their acknowledged lord in goods, services, and arms. Thus the empire never ended; and though its actual influence waxed and waned from time to time, deep respect remained for the unity it officially enshrined.

Thus, when Charlemagne, the king of the Franks, was crowned emperor by Pope Leo III in the church of Saint Peter's at Rome on Christmas Day in the year 800 – restoring at long last the Western imperial throne – there was less a sense of resurrecting a long lost legacy than of revitalizing a long cherished ideal.

At the core of the tenacious commitment to imperial unity in the West – against all apparent odds – was the acceptance of a common faith, a common heritage, and a common destiny. But there was more to it than that. Christendom was heralded, cherished, and venerated as a confederated republic – the kind of republic which preserves a universal hierarchy, maintains a common notion of justice, enforces a routine accountability, and joins arms for war or crusade.

To be sure, men differed on the issue of where the ultimate authority in this republic lay; some believed it lay with the emperor, others with the Pope, and still others with a representative council. Disputes over the proper structuring of the republic were often fierce. At various times, general councils met – such as those which convened in the Lateran, at Pisa, in Avignon, and at Basle – in an attempt to sort out such disputes peacefully. At other times, overlords took to arms in an attempt to sort them out forcefully. Yet through it all, a strong sense of unity remained intact – never did men fragment their loyalties with anything like what we today call nationalism.

As late as the end of the sixteenth century, the popular chronicler, Jacob Meyer, could say without a hint of hyperbole, "The Christian republic is a single kingdom, a house undivided: the wars which are waged between its subjects are a matter for great shame; they should not in truth be called wars, but base sedition."

Even so, while it was more than the fiction modern historians would like to make it, the empire republic of Christendom was simultaneously less than the fact that catholic idealists would like to make it – precisely because of the "inter-Nicene" warfare that Meyer so rues.

Such shameful bickering seems to have been inevitable however, integrally woven into the anarchic fabric of feudalism – a remarkably paradoxical system that happily decentralized the centralization of Christendom by means of the checks and balances, the separation of powers, and the tiered system of appeals and accountabilities that are the heart and soul of covenantalism.

Toward the end of the Roman regency in the fifth century, the mass-migration of Germanic tribes over the Rhine, into Gaul, and across the Pyrenees put an unbearable strain upon the imperial treasury. The administration of those outlying provinces simply outstripped the diminishing resources of Roman governance. Thus the emperor reluctantly entrusted the task of defending the borders, collecting the taxes, and keeping the peace to the barbarian chieftains and warlords who now lived there – making them his vassal allies. In return for their faithful obeisance, he granted them lands, titles, and authorities in hereditary perpetuity – they thus became kings, dukes, barons, marquises, and nobles.

This was the very simple beginning of what became the very complex feudal order which, in time, would dominate the affairs of men and movements throughout the medieval era. Ultimately, everyone within the society would have some sort of a covering of accountability and allegiance. Rather than allowing the West to become a progressively atomized and fragmented community, the federal nature of feudalism aimed at a genuine covenantal unity – with the various inter-related stations in life stacked like a giant woodpile.

What made the dynamic of feudalism actually work was the fact that this woodpile was personal in nature – not merely institutional. Thus, peasants related to their local lords, local lords related to dukes and princes, dukes and princes related to kings, and kings related to emperors or popes. Fidelity, chivalry, and were thus calculated on the basis of relationships to people not to governments, states, lands, or countries.

At least, that was the theory – but like nearly all good theories it was often discredited if not disproven in its practice.

Follow the confusing lineage of the royal families or the sagas of their anguished wars of succession and it is easy to see why the feudal system failed to live up to its vaunted ideals of balance, accountability, and harmony. Practical questions abounded: Can intermarriage merge provinces and kingdoms? Should lands be sub-divided among multiple heirs? Do illegitimate children have full – or even partial – inheritance rights? What happens when an overlord leaves no heirs? What if there is a dispute over the line of descent? Do two nobles with equally valid claims simply resort to war to determine supremacy? Can a lord forswear allegiance to one crown for another? Does his land then transfer to the new liege? What about annexations of pagan realms – are they to be accounted any differently? Or what about newly discovered territories? How are they to be assimilated? Can traitors be disinherited and dispossessed from their benefice? Are fiefdoms commodities to be traded or stewardships to be safeguarded? What is the status of the newly landed? If a family line ceases to exist, does the land escheat – or revert – to the overlord? Are nepotism, simony, and patronage legitimate means of transfer? In what ways do allodial farmers, merchants, clergy, and knights relate to their sovereigns?

No one ever adequately answered those questions – though many reformers, tyrants, and demagogues tried. As the centuries passed, the tangled web of royal intermarriage, the constant jostling of territories and titles, and the scandalous ethical degeneration of the church, only made matters worse.

By the time of Renaissance and the Reformation, the feudal system was hopelessly snarled in conflict and controversy. But it was still in place. It was still functioning. It still provided a semblance of Christian accord. Despite all its arcane quandaries, a pervading commitment to inter-personal honor, universal order, and abiding truth continued to fuel the fires of feudalism. Like faith, it was a perpetually defeated thing that survived all its conquerors.

Feudalism was forever a paradox. It was a romantic riddle. On the one hand it was marked by the greatest virtues of morality, charity, and selflessness; on the other hand it was marred by the flaming vices of perversity, betrayal, and avarice. It was often timid, monkish, and isolated; oftener still, it was bold, ostentatious, and adventurous. It was mystical; it was worldly. It was tenderhearted; it was cruel. It was ascetic; it was sensual. It was miserly; it was pretentious. It gripped men with a morbid superstition; it set them free with an untamed inquisitiveness. It exulted in pomp, circumstance, and ceremony; it cowered in poverty, tyranny, and injustice. It united men with faith, hope, and love; it divided them with war, pestilence, and prejudice. It was so unstable it could hardly have been expected to last a week; it was so stable that it actually lasted a millennium.

Whatever its strengths or weaknesses – and however much it paralleled our own strengths and weaknesses – the most obvious fact about the strange and unfamiliar feudal world of Medieval covenantalism is that it was indeed, strange and unfamiliar.

The periods that immediately followed Medievalism in the West were the Renaissance and the Enlightenment. Despite their many advances in art, music, medicine, science, and technology, these epochs were essentially nostalgic revivals of ancient pagan ideals and values. The dominating ideas of the times were classical humanism, pregnable naturalism, and antinomian individualism – or in other words: godlessness, materialism, and hedonism. Taking their cues primarily from ancient Greece and Rome, the leaders of the epoch were not so much interested in the Christian notion of progress as they were in the heathen ideal of innocence. Reacting to the artificialities and contrivances of the Medieval period, they dispatched the Christian consensus it had wrought with enervating aplomb. In short, they threw the baby out with the bath. Covenantal federalism was dispatched in favor of empire-building, the divine right of kings, and the imposition of arbitrary, ideological law.

Throughout history men have reacted instead of acted in times of crisis. They have sought to ameliorate an ill on the right hand by turning immediately and entirely to the left. They have tried to solve a problem in the citadels of the present by desecrating the foundations of the past. Driven by extremism, they have failed to see the moderating application of adjustments and alternatives.

When faced with the recalcitrance of feudal life, the immediate reaction of the people of the Renaissance and Enlightenment was to reject out of hand the very foundations of their Christian heritage. They abandoned federalism and covenantalism instead of actually building on that heritage for the future. Nothing was sacred any longer. Everything – every thought, word, and deed, every hope, dream, and aspiration, every tradition, institution, and relationship – was redefined.

No society can long stand without some ruling set of principles, some overriding values, or some ethical standard. Thus, when the men and women of the fifteenth through the eighteenth centuries threw off Christian mores, they necessarily went casting about for a suitable alternative. And so, Greek and Roman thought was exhumed from the ancient sarcophagus of paganism. Aristotle, Plato, and Pythagoras were dusted off, dressed up, and rehabilitated as the newly tenured voices of wisdom. Cicero, Seneca, and Herodotus were raised from the philosophical crypt and made to march to the tune of a new era.

Every forum, every arena, and every aspect of life began to reflect this newfound fascination with the pre-Christian past. Art, architecture, music, drama, literature, and every other form of popular culture began to portray the themes of classical humanism, pregnable naturalism, and antinomian individualism. They even began to extol the old pagan values as well – including the values of abortion, infanticide, abandonment, and exposure. A complete reversion took place. Virtually all the great advances in human freedom and social cohesion that the Medieval era brought were lost in just a few short decades.

It was not just the church that had become impotent, entirely unable to halt the rapid slide into the godlessness, materialism, and hedonism of the ancient pagan philosophies. Slowly but surely, the whole social fabric of Christendom was in very real jeopardy.

In the East, the fall of Constantinople and the subsequent captivity of much of Orthodoxy had made that once formidable force in Christendom of little influence. While in the West, rampant simony, monastic corruption, inquisitional fury, and infighting between orders had stymied the effectiveness of Catholicism. Meanwhile, popular culture took its nasty turn away from truth.

Thus, throughout the entire fifteenth century, cries for the reformation of both church and society came from every sector. From traditionalists to innovators, from mendicants to oblates, from magistrates to hierarchs, and from those who had vested interests to those entirely on the outside of the system, nearly everyone agreed that substantial reforms needed to take place. It was evident to even the most disinterested observer that the West would have to be dramatically revitalized if it were to survive, much less to thrive.

Virtually no one disagreed on the fact that the West needed to be reformed. What they disagreed on was what that reform should entail and how it was to be effected. In frustrated tension, dozens of competing factions, sects, schisms, rifts, rebellions, and divisions roiled just beneath the surface of the West's tenuous tranquility for decades. Finally, on October 31, 1517, those pent-up passions burst out into the open when an Augustinian monk named Martin Luther posted his "Ninety-Five Theses" on the door of the Castle Church in Wittenberg. In a single stroke, not one, but two momentous renewal movements were launched that at last were able to effect genuine reform within the church: the Protestant Reformation and the reaffirmation of covenantal principles to civil governance.

This is the essential historical and cultural framework out of which the *Magdeburg Confession* of 1550 was written. Against the backdrop of the centralizing totalitarianism of the Hapsburg hegemony, the newly revived Holy Roman Empire, the people of the little German town of Magdeburg, situated between Berlin and Hanover, not far from Brandenburg, determined to recover their federal, their covenantal, their Biblical culture.

Their confession of faith asserted that Biblical covenantalism was the principle by which men and nations might know the truth of the Gospel and thus afford hope for their souls, it was simultaneously the principle by which their cultural and political and social freedom might be won.

Ultimately, the font of covenantal ideas in the Magdeburg Confession flowed out into the reforming nations of the West: they were echoed in Calvin's Geneva; they helped shape Knox's Scotland, they were influential in Bucer's Strassburg; they laid the foundations of Cranmer's England; and as we have seen, they were central to the vision of the Founders of America's great experiment in liberty.

But for the same reasons that the Magdeburg pioneers had to recover the old Medieval principles of covenantal federalism by means of reformation, we need to pay heed to these ideas today. Western Civilization is once again in very real jeopardy. Freedom is once again threatened. Life, liberty, and opportunity are once again coming under the shadow of vested centralized powers and principalities.

We should all be grateful that this new translation, this new edition of the *Magdeburg Confession* is now available. By looking back at the essential notions upon which our freedoms were built we may yet be motivated and equipped to begin the process of reforming, restoring, and recovering. May it be so, Lord.

George Grant
Pastor of Presbyterian Parish Church
Lententide 2012
Franklin, TN

TRANSLATOR'S PREFACE

The present English translation of the Magdeburg Confession was made possible by one of the most wonderful benefits of technology: a digital copy of the Latin original is available from the Municher Sammlung, and accessible over the Internet. Thus this timely statement of the obligations of the lesser magistrate and of all Christians to resist tyranny has been lying "buried in plain sight." The illustrations of Michael Lotther's press are well worth seeing.

Nicolaus von Amsdorff wrote in the neo-Latin of the 16th century. His prose is simple in vocabulary, but with prolix multiple clauses and extended periods. For the sake of readability, I have occasionally broken his long sentences into shorter ones. I have attempted to render all terms consistently, so that parallel or anaphoric uses can be discerned in the text. Amsdorff's scripture references are in the margins of the Latin edition, but I have enclosed them in parentheses in the text. Occasionally Amsdorff has assumed that his reader will have knowledge of the Apocrypha or of historical names and events that are no longer common. I have attempted to supply this information in the notes.

I cannot lay claim to any great expertise in neo-Latin or Reformation history; my degree and all my previous published work are rather in ancient Greek philosophy. I undertook the project partly because, though now a member of the Reformed Episcopal Church, I was raised as a Lutheran; partly because I love the Lord and desire to use my language skills to advance His kingdom.

My greatest debt is to my mother Claudia: without her tireless discipline and teaching, I would never have learned Latin as a youth.

Thanks is also due to Pastor Matt Trewhella, whose generous patronage enabled me to devote time to the project this summer.

Finally, I would also like to thank Pastor Michael Bray for teaching me what liberty means, and for instilling in me a thirst for righteousness during my years under his teaching. He was also the one who suggested that I should take up the task.

Any deficiencies in the translation are of course mine.

Matthew Colvin
10th Sunday after Trinity
Mason, Ohio

Historical Setting

The historical context which led to the writing of the *Magdeburg Confession* began with Martin Luther posting his *95 Thesis* on the church door in Wittenburg in the year 1517. This sparked what is referred to by historians as *the Reformation*.

Luther and the Reformation were condemned in the *Edict of Worms* in 1521, which was presided over by the Emperor of the Holy Roman Empire, Charles V. The decree issued on May 25, 1521 declared in part:

> For this reason we forbid anyone from this time forward to dare, either by words or by deeds, to receive, defend, sustain, or favor the said Martin Luther. On the contrary, we want him to be apprehended and punished as a notorious heretic, as he deserves, to be brought personally before us, or to be securely guarded until those who have captured him inform us, whereupon we will order the appropriate manner of proceeding against the said Luther. Those who will help in his capture will be rewarded generously for their good work.

Luther was not arrested, and in fact, was seized and protected by Prince Frederick III of Saxony. This act of defiance and protection by a lesser magistrate proved important to the development of the lesser magistrate doctrine as detailed in the *Magdeburg Confession*.

Charles V had a difficult time upholding the Edict in Germany because of the defiance and protection of several German princes towards their citizens, and because of encroachments made upon his empire by the French and the Turks.

After the *Diet of Augsburg* in 1530, which was intended to ease tensions between Roman Catholic and Protestant rulers in Germany, Luther was concerned that Charles V might very well enforce the Edict of Worms militarily. This threat prompted him to write his *Warning to his Dear German People* which was published in 1531 and contained three parts. The *Magdeburg Confession* was modeled after Luther's *Warning*, also containing three parts.

In 1531, the *Schmalkaldic League* was formed by Prince Phillip of Hesse and Prince John Frederick I of Saxony, the two most powerful Protestant rulers at the time. The League was a defensive religious alliance, with the members pledging to defend each other should their territories be attacked by Charles V.

The *League* existed unmolested by Charles V for 15 years.

In June 1546, just 4 months after Martin Luther had died, Charles V entered into an agreement with Pope Paul III in order to curb the spread of the Reformation. The agreement stated, in part:

> In the name of God and with the help and assistance of his Papal Holiness, his Imperial Majesty should prepare himself for war, and equip himself with soldiers and everything pertaining to warfare against those who objected to the Council [of Trent], against the Smalcaldic League, and against all who were addicted to the false belief and error in Germany, and that he do so with all his power and might, in order to bring them back to the old faith and to the obedience of the Holy See.

Charles called together his magistrates and military forces to take coercive action against the Reformers in Germany.

On July 4, 1546, the leaders of the Schmalkaldic League gathered to take defensive action by making a pre-emptive strike against Charles' forces. These efforts were thwarted however when Maurice, Duke of Saxony, switched sides and joined forces with Charles, having accepted an offer from Charles to be named the new Elector upon John Frederick's defeat. Maurice hated John Frederick, Elector of Saxony.

The decisive battle of the war took place on April 24, 1547, at the battle of Muhlberg. The Schmalkaldic League forces were

Temporary agree between German Catholics + Protestants—May 1548

HISTORICAL SETTING   at Diet of Augsburg
Forced by Charles V - Catholic view!

defeated, and both Phillip of Hesse and John Frederick of Saxony
were captured and imprisoned.

The following year, after a further Diet of Augsburg, Charles
imposed his *Augsburg Interim* on May, 15, 1548. This law was intended
to coerce Protestants to readopt traditional Roman Catholic beliefs,
practices, and rule.

The *Interim* demanded that the Lutherans restore the number of
sacraments (which the Lutherans had reduced to two) to seven, and
that the churches restore a number of Roman ceremonies, doctrines,
and practices which had been discarded by the Lutheran reformers,
including transubstantiation. The decree also called for the rejection
of the doctrine of justification by faith alone, and required that the
Pope be acknowledged as the head of the Church by divine right and
that the churches receive again the authority of the Roman bishops.
In concession to the Lutherans, the *Interim* allowed for the marriage
of clergy, and that the laity be given both elements (bread and wine)
in communion.

Even though Phillip Melancthon, friend and heir-apparent
of Luther, was willing to compromise these issues for the sake of
peace, the *Augsburg Interim* was rejected by a significant number of
Lutheran pastors and theologians. Hundreds of pastors were imprisoned, exiled or executed for refusing to follow the regulations of the
Interim.

Another friend of Luther's felt differently than Melancthon
however, namely, Nicholas von Amsdorff. He was with Luther during the Diet of Worms. He also participated in the planning of the
protective action taken by the lesser magistrate, Prince Frederick
III, on behalf of Luther. He was presently in Magdeburg and would
remain there throughout the seige, and would be the first signer on
the *Confession*.

Only one city in all of Germany stood against the Interim –
Magdeburg. Here the magistrates protected the people and stood
against religious and political tyranny. They upheld God's Law, Word,
and Gospel. While all of Christendom went along with these sanc-
tions in order to preserve their own well-being – the lone city which
stood in opposition was Magdeburg.

As tensions mounted, the pastors of Magdeburg wrote a defense of their position for standing in defiance of Charles V and his unjust Interim. They published their *Confession and Defense of the Pastors and Other Ministers of the Church of Magdeburg* in April 1550.

In October of 1550, Charles' forces, led by Maurice, surrounded the city. The people of Magdeburg burned everything outside the city walls and closed the gates. The seige of Magdeburg had begun.

It was this historical setting in which the pastors of Magdeburg took their stand in fealty to Christ.

THE CONFESSION AND DEFENSE OF THE PASTORS AND OTHER MINISTERS OF THE CHURCH OF MAGDEBURG

13th of April in the year 1550

Psalm 18:
I spoke of your testimonies in the sight of kings,
and was not put to shame.

Romans 13
Rulers are not a terror for good works, but for evil.

Acts 9
Saul, Saul, why are you persecuting me? It is hard for you
to kick against the goad.

Printed at Magdeburg by Michael Lotther
[Replica of the actual title page from the original Magdeburg
Confession in 1550]

PREFACE

There can be no doubt that God by his great kindness raised up Dr. Martin Luther as a third Elijah, in order that he might reveal in these last days (according to His published prophecies) the Man of Sin, the Son of Perdition, the Antichrist, ruling in Rome in the Temple of God; likewise, to destroy him by the Spirit of the mouth of Christ, and to rebuild the entire doctrine of His Son. Therefore, since God had raised Luther up for this exceedingly difficult task, He also equipped him at the same time by the Holy Spirit with a superior understanding of the sacred Scriptures, with singular strength of faith in his heart like an immovable rock, and with lively skill in his mouth for teaching and arguing. He kindled his mind with the most ardent zeal for the House of God and filled it with the utmost hatred of the Pope and of all impiety. He gave him an audience in a great part of the Roman Empire, and among certain other kingdoms and peoples, and He gloriously defended both his person and his cause right up to the last moment of his life. Plainly He brought it about that whatever task He had commanded, Luther happily undertook it, more happily saw it through, and brought it to the happiest completion[1] despite the raging gates of the world and of Hell.

And God has blessed this man, His prophet, with so many notable testimonies and favorable outcomes of his labors that in the end they cannot be counted. Although the fortunes both of the man himself and of this entire doctrine seemed especially to be on the wane, almost not less than they are at this very moment, especially because supporters in the recent case were still poor and weak, while

---

1 Amsdorff, with his escalating *triad feliciter, felicius, quam felicissime* puns on the dual meanings of *felix,* which has reference both to Luther's willing and cheerful obedience, and to the successful outcome of his efforts..

its enemies were very numerous and powerful, and moreover they were banded together for this purpose, that they were not willing to rest before they had Caesar persecuting with his fury, and that they were ready to expend their own resources and life to extirpate this entire doctrine – nevertheless, God more fully stirred up the spirit of a few leaders and states to present by their own hand the articles of the doctrine, made plain by Luther, before the senate of the entire Roman Empire, at the greatest risk to themselves. Because God so marvelously determined the outcome, the poor sheep straightway stopped the jaws and mouth of the opposing wolves by this confession of the truth.

For when their theologians had been ordered to write a refutation of the confession produced by a few Lutherans, those men not only did it with difficulty and timidly, but also so clumsily and without the true foundation of the word of God, that once the refutation met the ears of those in the senate of the Empire who were expecting a plain refutation of the heresy alleged by them, it testified greatly of the emptiness of the popish doctrine. Nor did that doctrine dare to go forward into the light, though we urged it. And finally, since their own leaders were demanding it, they admitted that they were priests of Baal, that they were not able to defeat the Lutheran religion by the word of God, and that maybe they could by the Church Fathers.

These and many other similar things were done at Augsburg in the convention that took place 20 years ago.[2] They are known to very many people who either were there themselves, or read written accounts by others.

The cause of Luther, therefore, has always been victorious from the beginning, both then in that assembly, and afterwards in every gathering for debate, and remains hitherto unvanquished by testimonies and arguments from the Word of God.

The truth, moreover, is not defeated by arms. Victory by arms is neither able to change anything about the truth, nor does it always accompany the truth. We know that the prophets, Christ, and the apostles, all died in a similar way and in a similar cause. We know the ordinance of God, according to which, by suffering unjust violence,

---

2 In the margin, Amsdorff writes: "See the book of Luther entitled "Warnung an seine lieben Deutschen," near the beginning."

tortures,[3] and death, we are conformed to the image of His own Son. And so there is no reason from their recent (sc. military) victory either that the enemies should condemn the cause of Luther, or that they should vaunt themselves overmuch, or that the pious should grow faint.

The cause of the prophets, of Christ, and of the apostles first truly began to emerge in oppression, and they themselves after their death began to be more glorious. For this purpose God placed his prophets and apostles, that they should go forth bearing fruit and that their fruit should remain, and that He himself might display power in weakness, life in death, glory in shame, His planting in their uprooting.

And so Luther, although dead, both lives forever himself and the fruit of his work, as if it were a dead man, also lives, and shall live, and shall flourish in all ages and among still more nations. Nor shall the Antichrist ever regain his earlier strength, as Daniel, Paul, and John bear witness, howsoever much he shall try.[4]

But the confession of the doctrine of Luther, which is the doctrine of Christ Himself, as it was first made at Augsburg, with great faith and glory of those who confess it, has now at Augsburg been cast off again in a horrible crime against conscience by the majority of princes and German states who were broken only by the outcome of the recent war.[5] It was necessary for them to be accused publicly of this public crime, both individually by their own pastors, and as a group by their superintendents, and for them to give proofs of their repentance publicly. So long as that does not happen, there is no remaining place of forgiveness with God, nor shall the plague be removed from the families of their leaders, nor from the rest of Germany the apostate.

Or is it not really a rejection of the articles of the Augsburg Confession to subject doctrine itself and the Church to the authority

---

3 Literally "crosses" (cruces).

4 Amsdorff is making an eschatological pronouncement, identifying the Pope with the Man of Sin and seeing the Reformation as the dawn of the millenium.

5 Amsdorff refers to the Emperor Charles V's military victories over the Schmalkaldic League, which resulted in the so-called "Augsburg Interim," proclaimed at the 1548 Diet of Augsburg, where the Emperor attempted to reinstate Roman Catholic worship, albeit with some concessions.

of the Antichrist? That no further mention should be made of the Augsburg Confession either by voice or in writing, but that the memory and appearance of that confession should be effaced by a contrary label and an indifferent appearance? For it to be cursed by some men, unto the pleasure of our enemies and the contempt of the Gospel? That although Luther has been the chosen instrument of God for laying bare this gospel against the Antichrist, the churches of Christ should be subjected to that very Antichrist? In all these things, we see a true rejection before God of the entire Augsburg Confession, and with this also a rejection of Christ himself, so neither Caesar with his bishops and popes has interpreted these indications in any other way, nor is our side, especially the foreign churches, able to interpret them in any other way. Also many good men are thus moved to reject the Doctrine of these articles, and enemies are thereby motivated to blaspheme this doctrine and persecute it all the more.

Therefore, even if these states and those whom they have consenting in this apostasy have really rejected the Augsburg Confession, and by this rejection or harlotry with the Antichrist have made all of Christ, the Gospel, and the rest of religion all no less useless to themselves than have other fornicators of this world who do not repent – nonetheless, there still remain some poor vestiges of states, however weak, and of other pious persons even under the apostates, who agree with us in this, and who also retain the articles of the doctrine which was handed down to us by the ministry of Luther, and in these articles they confess Christ like the thief on the cross. Since our magistrates and the church of this city are among them, to the point that our enemies themselves profess to be assailing the remnants of this confession among us, we judge that it is part of our duty, since by the kindness of God we seem to be singled out from the whole church to have a voice that is still free, that we publicly put forth something to vindicate in some way the revealed doctrine of the Gospel from this unjust oppression.

So in this writing, first of all we shall only repeat – we shall not argue – the articles of doctrine made plain by Luther and set forth at Augsburg as Christian, orthodox, and catholic, and so far unconquered, as those which agree with the doctrine of the Apostles and Prophets, with the Apostles', Nicene, and Athanasian creeds, and with the purer church of all ages. At the same time, we shall add some things along the way, since there is a dissent from this timeless consensus of doctrine by the papists, Interimists,[6] and Adiaphorists,[7] and likewise the Anabaptists, Sacramentarians, [8] and similar fanatics – from all of whom we have most distantly withdrawn ourselves.

Secondly, we shall prove that the preservation of this doctrine is necessary for a godly magistrate, and that the dissent of a godly magistrate is just, even against a superior one who is using arms to force the rightly instituted churches of Christ to defect from the acknowledged truth and turn to idolatry.

In the third section of this little book, we shall warn all the pious of all churches, both magistrates and subjects, and we shall point out, not only how great a crime those men are committing who bring help to our persecutors of this doctrine and of the Church against us, but also how those who fail to aid us are not without fault; and how both these things, the opposition to us, and the desertion of us, will be dangerous to their bodily health and their eternal salvation, and to their entire posterity.

In drawing out these propositions, since we desire to offer insult to no one, we shall even freely spare those who do us harm, so far as the nature of the matters which we must speak about allows, and so far as the very reason of our task allows us to be spared by sparing them. If anyone still seizes upon anything in this writing said rather harshly against himself or against others, let him consider only what the subject matter is, and that in our calling, we had to put the glory of God ahead of the glory of men, just as he had to in his own calling; and that we had to value the health of this mortal body less than the eternal salvation of our souls; and that the preservation of a few of His own members is dearer to Christ than the entire remaining world of the impious, with all its trappings and gifts.

---

6 i.e. supporters of the Augsburg Interim.

7 By "Adiaphorists", Amsdorff means followers of Melanchthon's compromises with Rome concerning the number of sacraments and certain Roman distinctives in worship.

8 i.e. Zwinglians.

THE PRINCIPAL ARTICLES OF CHRISTIAN DOCTRINE

In order that the whole may be briefer, we shall arrange the entirety of Christian doctrine in 7 chapters:

i.   Of God and the distinction of the persons.
ii. Of creation, of the cause of sin, and the chief kinds of sin.
iii. Of the Law.
iv. Of the Gospel and Justification.
v.   Of the Sacraments.
vi. Of the Church and its ministers, and of the power of the Church and its ministers.
vii. Of polity and economy, and of the power of each.

The reason for this arrangement is the following: first, because all knowledge about God is either knowledge of His nature or of His will, disclosed either in the creation or in His revealed Word, especially so that the Church might be brought into being, by the ministry of the Law, of the Gospel, and of the Sacraments through men called to this ministry; and also because economy and polity ought to be subservient chiefly to the generating of the Church, or at the very least, for the civil society of men among themselves, when they do not attain any other end.

But since we have here set forth only a brief and bare exposition of the articles of doctrine, as a confession of our faith, we refer the reader to the numerous writings of the man of God Dr. Martin Luther, and of others from among of his friends, from which he may gain a fuller treatment and firm foundations. And we ourselves, as often as is necessary, are prepared to set forth the sources and true foundation of this whole doctrine and of our confession from the Scriptures of the prophets and apostles and from the agreement of the ancient Church and the purer church of nearly all ages.

OF GOD AND THE DISTINCTION OF THE PERSONS,

CHAPTER 1

Concerning the nature of God, we declare and teach against heretics ancient and modern from the certain Word of God, according to the declaration of the Apostolic, Nicene, and Athanasian Creeds, that there is one God, the Father, Son, and Holy Spirit, that is, three persons, indivisible, intelligent, and incommunicable, of the same substance, of infinite power and glory, equally from eternity.

Likewise we confess that the Son was made man, conceived of the Holy Spirit, born of the virgin Mary, so that our Lord Jesus Christ should be true God and true man, with his body and rational soul thus united with the eternal Word of the Father in one person, because by this union Christ is God and man, but by His free or voluntary humiliation and *kenosis*,[9] He really suffered, was crucified, died, and was buried; He descended to the dead according to the will of the Father; on the third day He was made alive again and ascended into heaven, and sits at the right hand of the Heavenly Father, ruling with equal power with the Father for all eternity; Who shall come again with majesty to do universal judgment on the entire human race. And when the resurrection of all the dead has happened, He shall repay each one according to his works; that is, to those who have repented and trusted in Him, He shall give possession of the inheritance of God in eternal life; but the rest, the impenitent and unbelieving, He shall subject together with the Devil to the penalty of damnation and eternal death.

---

9   Emptying Himself. (Philippians 2:7)

OF CREATION, OF THE CAUSE OF SIN, AND WHAT SIN IS,

CHAPTER 2

Through this Son, our Lord Jesus Christ, God, in order that He might manifest Himself in this way, and that He might be worshipped, established all things in the beginning, both bodily and spiritual natures, not out of any pre-existing material, but only by His commanding. And things thus both came into being and are preserved today, by the life-giving Holy Spirit.

And although all things were very good when God had created them, nonetheless evil soon afterwards entered in – that is, sin and death, not indeed from God, but from the will of the Devil and of man. For since these had been created in the image of God, in wisdom, righteousness, and eternal life, and endowed also with the freedom of doing good according to the will of God, they soon used the same freedom for evil against God, and thus they destroyed themselves, since God was not making the opposite happen, or forcing them to do otherwise. Thus the deed is understood to be in man.

As soon as our parents were persuaded by the Devil to eat from the fruit of the forbidden tree, God in His wrath turned Himself away from them by His righteous judgment. By this turning away of the grace and help of God, all His gifts were at the same time diminished and confused in man, and in the rest of created nature on account of man. And by this diminution and confusion of His gifts, contrary motions soon entered in. And the Devil, already having gained power against man and against this lower world[10], sprinkled more stains over a large part of his abandoned human

---

10 Amsdorff alludes to the sublunary sphere in the Aristotelian/medieval world-picture. For a helpful introduction to this topic, cf. C.S. Lewis, The Discarded Image.

nature, increased the shadows in his mind and his obstinacy against God, and the disorder in his remaining lower powers. And so God immediately punished sin with sin, by the power of the Devil, by disasters of every kind in body and soul, and last of all by death, – that is, because of sin, man was made subject to bodily and eternal death.

And since our first parents were now this way after their sin, they did not afterwards beget anyone else than those similar to themselves, in their own image, not in the image of God, since the gifts still remaining in man's corrupted nature degenerated even more with the progress of generations. And so all the men who descend from Adam by natural generation are conceived and born together with sin, i.e. they are born objects of wrath and of God's judgment, liable to the power of the Devil and of death, and that both on account of the actual sin committed by our first parents, and on account of their own corruption of their nature, by which they have no share in true knowledge, fear, faith, or love of God and neighbor; by which they are lovers of themselves, full of error, worry, mistrust, doubt, hatred of God, wicked lusts, and words and deeds contrary to God – to the point that nothing is left in any part of all of man descended by nature by which he might be able to please God or to receive grace and life. The psychikos man[11] is still in some way able to achieve upright works in a civil manner, whence arise shadows of the virtues and external discipline even among the Gentiles.

PROB   Two errors of the Papists are especially at odds with this whole doctrine. The first is the error by which they deny that the vice inherent in our nature, our revolt and concupiscence, is sin in itself, but is, as they say, the penalty and kindling of sin, which inclines a man to sinning and easily takes up sin. The other error concerns the

---

11 (Here and elsewhere I have left Amsdorff's Greek words and phrases in the text). The term comes from 1 Cor. 15:44, where *"soma psychikon"* has often been mistranslated "a natural body", so that Amsdorff's *"homo psychikos"* would be rendered as "the natural man." But this is incorrect, for Greek has a good word for "nature", *physis*, and it is not used here. Strictly speaking, *"soma psychikon"* means "a body animated by a psyche," – a soul descended from Adam, who "became a living psyche" (Gen. 2:7 LXX); in contrast to a soma *pneumatikon* – "a body animated by the Spirit" of Christ. For exegesis of 1 Corinthians 15 and further explanation of this point, cf. N. T. Wright, The Resurrection of the Son of God.

goodness of the depraved nature, that man is able either himself by his own natural powers to satisfy the Law of God, or to deserve grace by congruent merit.[12]

---

12 The phrase *"mereri gratiam de congruo"* is a reference to the doctrine of the Council of Trent (Sess. VI, cap. xvi). The distinction between congruent and condign merit was a chief issue in debates between Luther and Johann Eck.

OF THE LAW,

CHAPTER 3

Just as God in the beginning made Himself known through the creation, so thereafter he made Himself known both by His revealed word before and after the fall of man, through commandments and promises by which man might exercise obedience and faith toward God. Furthermore, the same will of God written by nature in men's hearts, but obscured by the progress of time in the first centuries, God afterwards set forth again in the Law given through Moses, so that in every age men might have the certain witness of the word of God, from which to know what they ought to do, what they ought not to do, and how they ought to conduct themselves toward God and toward each other – namely, that they ought to be pure in heart, and ought to render perpetual and entire obedience, external and internal, without evil affections. To those who render this obedience, He also adds the promise of perpetual salvation in this life and the life to come, and against sinners He threatens temporal and eternal punishments,

God did not, however, want this will of his to exist in the Law so that men by doing the Law might be able to attain righteousness and life by its works, or that they ought to climb up it to attain them, but so that they, despairing of their own merits and terrified by the sight of their sins and the wrath of God toward their sins, and deeply mortified by the Law, might seek and receive from the gospel freedom from sin, from the wrath of God, and from death, and a share in Christ; and so that they might have righteousness and life through the same; and so that afterwards they might also be diligent to be grateful by obedience to these very precepts. When they have been justified by faith to begin this obedience, they are reborn through the Holy Spirit.

God wants even the impious or unregenerate to be governed by an outward discipline in this civil society. Therefore He has ordained and related penalties and rewards of various sorts, whether through ministers of the word, magistrates, and heads of households, or whether He Himself punishes the obstinate without these ministers. And on the other hand He does good in this life to upright men, so that He may in this way bring about and keep a certain discipline in the outward habits of our life.

Although through Moses God also gave certain ceremonial and judicial laws in addition to the Decalogue, they were imposed for a limited time until Christ, and do not bind Christian churches now except insofar as there are certain natural things in them. The Ten Words, however, are perpetual laws, and binding on all men of all times, sacred as well as profane, as has been said earlier.

Against this doctrine of the Law there are many very great errors of the papists.

1. They corrupt the Law, denying that the deficiency of reverence, faith, joy, and similar defects in the nature of man are sins. Likewise they teach that man is able to satisfy the Law of God as far as the substance of his deeds, and that God is content with outward discipline.

2. They twist the Law when from its commands about not taking revenge, about our lack of ability, and other things like that, they make schemes and works of supererogation and perfection; likewise when they prefer the choice of a monastic life and other human traditions rather than the works commanded in the divine Law. And although the Interimists and Adiaphorists no longer speak this way about these works, nonetheless because they both restore these very works of human tradition (sc. certain Roman sacraments and ceremonies) and likewise the power from which those impious opinions arose (sc. the supremacy of the pope), they sufficiently confirm and abet the impious opinions themselves as well.

3. The papists impiously teach that the Law was given for justification and life, that is, so that we might be justified before God by the works of the Law, and so that we might merit eternal life.

4. Just as the Anabaptists partly abolish the Law, removing civil office and judgments and the distinction between the dominions,

so the papists maim and distort the Law, forbidding marriage to priests, and denying that political and economic works ought to be cultivated among believers.

5. Just as in our day certain madmen have wickedly attempted to call back into the churches of Christians the judicial laws of Moses by divine authority, and as the Roman Popes by their affectation of ceremonial rules have instituted their Papacy and the sacrifice of the Mass, so the Antinomians by their pernicious impiety have wanted to remove from the Church the proper and especial use of moral commandments, by which the moral law accuses, terrifies, and condemns sinners against their conscience.

OF THE GOSPEL AND
JUSTIFICATION,

CHAPTER 4

The gospel is the doctrine concerning the will of God towards us in Christ Jesus, which will was first published in Paradise immediately after the fall of our first parents. Thereafter God repeated and illustrated it, both Himself and through the prophets, and finally through His Son, because it is only through Him, and on His account alone that He desires to receive those who repent and believe in the name of His Son.

There are, therefore, two parts of this doctrine. One is about the benefits belonging to Christ, the other about the application of these benefits to us. The benefits belonging to Christ are chiefly these: that by His merit alone we have deliverance from Sin, from the wrath of God, and from death; that we have righteousness, adoption, the Holy Spirit, and eternal life. The application is by faith alone in adults who repent, in this way:

When God remits or does not impute sin to whatever man He wants, there is joined together with that forgiveness absolution from the penalty of eternal death, just as in court forgiveness of a fault has joined with it forgiveness of any civil penalty.

But it happens more fully in the judgment of God, since when they have been absolved from blame and eternal punishment on account of His Son, God also at the same time imputes to them the entire righteousness of His Son. That is, He pronounces them to have all the virtues of His Son, and thus to be righteous before Him with the righteousness of another as though it were their own, just as in the forgiveness of guilt and eternal punishment He accepts the alien satisfaction of His Son just as if they had made their own satisfaction individually. This is the second benefit the judge gives to the accused, although he is not able to present it to him on his own —namely, to pronounce him in the same way righteous, that is, furnished with all virtues – him who a little while before had been accused of the greatest crimes. He is able to adopt him into His Son; and this, moreover, is just what God has done: He adopts as sons those whom He receives into grace.

And so, absolved from sin and eternal punishment, they are at the same time righteous before God with the imputed righteousness of His Son, and are also themselves sons of God; and they have a right to life and eternal salvation by a double title: They have it as their inheritance by adoption, for as sons of God they are heirs of eternal life. They also have it as their wages by the merit, not of their own righteousness, but of the alien righteousness of Christ. For life is given, just as was promised, also on account of the righteousness of the Law, according to that saying, "He who does these things shall live by them": Christ has done that righteousness and has gifted it to us by imputation through faith. Therefore we also have life by this imputation of His righteousness.

But God has absolved no one from sin and death, and made him righteous and a son and an heir of eternal life, unless He first gives him the Holy Spirit Who by the Word and sacraments moves and directs the heart to the true recognition or taste of sin and of the wrath of God, to trust in Christ the mediator that lays hold of these goods according to the promise in Him, namely the forgiveness of sins, righteousness, adoption and life. By this trust alone the heart itself is also made more fully alive by eternal life; it conceives a new and true consolation, light, hatred of sin, love of righteousness, and likewise new strength for resisting sin and for doing the works of inherent righteousness[13] according to the Law – not so that a man might now for the first time be justified before God through these works, since he earlier becomes righteous by the alien righteousness of the Son of God; nor that he might be able to do works pleasing to God, unless he has been earlier justified in this way; nor even that he might merit life by these works, since he has a prior right to this

---

13 By "inherent righteousness" Amsdorff means the new habitus of the regenerate, in contrast to the alien righteousness of Christ, which does not by itself produce good works in the sinner.

life, since he is a son and righteous with the righteousness of the son of God – but for this reason, that he might present to God the obedience and honor which is owed Him for the gifts of creation and redemption in His Son; and so that he might not lose these gifts again once they have been received, and slide back again into the wrath of God and death. And so Christ Himself by His own Word and the Holy Spirit, who is efficacious by the Word and Sacraments, begins regeneration, advances it in the mature, and completes it, so that just as all the glory is His in the merit of our salvation, and His is the gift of Word and Sacraments, so also in the application of His merit, or regeneration, which comes about in repentance, the beginning, middle, and end might be all of Him. And this is the "drawing" of the Father about which Christ speaks in John 6.[14]

Furthermore, the will that has been regenerated by the Holy Spirit is able either to use the gifts that have been accepted, or not to use them. And the gifts themselves increase in those who use them, and they have other rewards, corporal and spiritual, in this life and in the life to come. In those who do not use them, or who do otherwise, the gifts that are present are diminished and removed along with the Holy Spirit. There are very frequent passages in the gospel urging this use of the gifts of the Holy Spirit, by which the reborn are commanded to live now according to the Spirit; to put to death the works of the flesh; and to do works of righteousness.

And although in the conversion or regeneration of adults the Holy Scriptures describe three principal movements, namely contrition, faith, and new obedience, nonetheless those movements themselves occur together in different ways, and the forgiveness of sins, justification, adoption and life are not ascribed to anything but faith alone, not even to the other two movements, either separately or together. For faith alone accepts Christ as the mediator, and His benefits promised in the Word; and therefore faith alone frees a man from sin and death, justifies him and makes him alive, not by reason of its own dignity or merit, but that of Christ, on whom alone it rests and envelopes the whole man.

It does not therefore exclude contrition and the other virtues, that they should not be present, but it excludes them from merit and

---

14 John 6:44: "No one can come to Me unless the Father who sent me draws him."

from the receiving of the benefits of Christ, yet so that faith itself neither exists, nor can exist, without them. For faith is properly the justification of a conscience that acknowledges its own unrighteousness, the comforting of a terrified conscience, the making alive of a conscience killed by the Law, by the sight of its sins and the wrath of God; nor does such faith have any place or exist in those who are untroubled. This faith is also a regeneration to new and eternal righteousness and life, and without at least the beginning of this new righteousness and life, that faith which boasts of Christ and the forgiveness of sins is hypocrisy, not faith, giving birth to death, not life.

And since this regeneration of a new man is only begun in this life through baptism, and only the first fruits of the Spirit are given, not the tenth, therefore the entire obedience is still imperfect, and there are vestiges of the old man remaining after baptism in those who are sanctified; there remain also failings and concupiscence against the Law of God, which are also really evils, and remain sin, just as the Apostle also names sin, that is, things by which God is really offended; by which He is also angered. But He is not angered at, nor on that account does he condemn a person who believes in His Son, one who lives with a good conscience, not according to the flesh, but according to the Spirit, just as a judge who acquits a thief nonetheless always hates the crime itself and judges it worthy of hanging, and wants the acquitted man to refrain from any similar theft in the future, lest he be snatched away again to punishment.

I have faithfully reproduced this summary of the teaching of Scripture about the whole business of justification. There are nearly infinite corruptions of it among the papists, so we shall take note of only a few chief errors, in order that the difference between the two doctrines may be clearer.

1. First, they have transformed the gospel back into the Law by their invention concerning the precepts of the gospel, or "new Law."

2. Removing the promise of free reconciliation for the sake of Christ, not only have they removed the proper difference between Law and Gospel, but they have nearly utterly done away with the benefit of Christ and the Gospel, and

attributed them to their works. They removed from Christ his proper glory, and from quivering consciences their necessary comfort.

3. Nevertheless, lest they make Christ entirely useless, they have ascribed to Him the merit of "first grace", by which, when we have been absolved of the alien guilt of our first parents, and prepared by infused dispositions, by faith, hope, and charity, we may afterwards merit for ourselves forgiveness of sins, righteousness and eternal life, by the works of the law – not of God, but – of human traditions.

4. They have taught that "first grace" is applied by works of repentance *ex opere operato*.[15]

5. They have made contrition, confession, and satisfaction the parts of repentance. And since they attribute to them not only the merit of "first grace," but also of remission of guilt and penalty, they completely bury faith and Christ.

6. In confession they impiously require the enumeration of all sins as though it were required by divine right: they impiously drive out contrition as sufficing.

7. They invent the idea that for the contrite and those who have confessed, eternal penalties are changed into penalties of purgatory, and these, they claim, are paid for by canonical satisfactions, that is, by works of human traditions imposed by the power of the keys; and they say that these satisfactions themselves are also bought with money via indulgences.

8. Although the Augsburg book (sc. the terms of the interim), in its chapter on Redemption through Christ, wishes to seem to attribute all the merit of forgiveness, righteousness, and salvation to the free mercy of God and to Christ, nevertheless it afterwards takes it away again and defines merit proper in terms of the works of the Law, in exactly the same way as the Papists did above. For since the inherent righteousness, faith, hope, and charity which Christ has merited and fosters in us by the Holy Spirit does not liberate, justify, and save us except by use, which use is properly ours, then we certainly

---

15 *Ex opere operato* - literally, "from the work worked". i.e. works of repentance bring about "first grace" the way a hot iron burns.

also have the glory of our justification and salvation before God, rather than Christ Himself, and we are basically justified and saved by the works of the Law, and plainly not by Christ Himself.

9. Both the Papists and the Interimists understand faith here only as assent to the history concerning Christ, and the other things which it is necessary to know: they perforce do away with the "full persuasion and boldness" of trust in Christ with their contrary doctrine, by which they order us to doubt and to depend on our inherent righteousness.

10. The Adiaphorists also depart widely from the purity of the Apostolic doctrine, and from the Augsburg Confession in this article. First, when they do not hand down the distinction between inherent righteousness, or the righteousness of works, or the righteousness of our own on the one hand; and on the other hand, alien righteousness, namely the righteousness of Christ imputed by faith – in doing this, they leave out the principal nub of this controversy in their explanation, and so they confuse these two righteousnesses, which ought to be distinguished. Second, when in their zeal they cast away the exclusive doctrine (that a man is justified by faith alone), and likewise when they begin to say with the adversaries that works are necessary for salvation, they confirm these two errors of our adversaries: that we are just as much righteous by our remaining virtues before God as we are righteous by faith; and that works are able to merit eternal life. Third, they themselves set up a certain glory of their own before God, if a man is able by some power of his own to follow the Holy Spirit who calls him, before regeneration or the movement of the Holy Spirit.

11. Although both the Interimists and Adiaphorists mutter some old nonsense about repentance, nonetheless the Interimists retain the core of all the old abominations. And since the Adiaphorists restore all the papistical "parts" of penance and the bishops (those wolves) to the churches, in the end, they shall not be able to prohibit the impious opinions of the papists even if they should wish to do so; nor will the

interpretation of those sophistries rest with them, but with our adversaries.

12. Concerning the remaining weakness in the saints after baptism, the error of the papists is manifest: they deny that that weakness is sin, and they also teach that the saints are able to be without sin.

13. Here we also condemn the Novatians who deny repentance to those who fall away after baptism. And we condemn the Anabaptists and their ilk who boast in enthusiasm, or who lead men astray to new revelations or other things of this sort, away from the Word and Sacraments, through which alone God is effective to salvation. And if anything else is at odds with the doctrine of justification outlined above, we judge it to be entirely foreign to the opinion of Holy Scripture, and opposed to the glory of Christ and the salvation of men.

- a tolerant conduct of beliefs

- a Xian protestant theological theory that certain titles and actions are matters of indifference in religion since they are not forbidden by scriptures.

See Adiaphora in Reformation History
and
Considerations for today"

ON THE SACRAMENTS,

CHAPTER 5

For the application of the benefits of Christ, which happens only by faith, the sacraments serve along with the Word. These sacraments, as Augustine says, are nothing other than the Word visible, that is, just as the promise of the benefits of Christ is offered first to the ears through the Word, so later it is offered also to the rest of the senses through the external signs of the sacraments, through which the Holy Spirit is equally effective to stir up and sharpen faith, so that the hearts may be able to believe the promise more firmly, helped by these, as it were, signs of the things promised, and that they may individually be able to consider the promised benefits as applying to themselves, the ones to whom they have been applied in this way. And so, without this faith, the sacraments do not benefit the one receiving them, but rather, are harmful to him.

This is the chief and proper use of the sacraments. At the same time, the sacraments are also marks and true works of confession, by which not only are pagans, Jews, and excommunicated persons distinguished from the Church, but also in the outward society of the Church true members are distinguished from false ones, that is, they are thereby distinguished from despisers and Epicureans.

Next, three things are required for the substance of each sacrament: first, a promise of grace concerning the benefits of Christ; second, an institution by God and a commandment; third, a thing[16] and an external action. Augustine sums up these essential attributes briefly under the label of "word" and "element" when he says, "let the word be added to the element, and a sacrament is made."

Against this true exposition about sacraments is opposed the impious teaching of the Anabaptists, whereby they deny the true

---

16 Thing is *res* in the Latin. Amsdorff means what later theologians will designate as the invisible and spiritual grace of the sacraments.

efficacy of the sacraments for salvation, and do away with the true and proper use of them. Also opposed to it is the error of the papists, who attribute, it is true, efficacy to them, but only ex opere operato, that is, without trust laying hold of the promise and applying the benefits of Christ to the person using the sacrament. There are, moreover, only three sacraments of this kind that we describe, instituted by Christ in the New Testament: to wit, baptism, the Lord's Supper, and Absolution.

OF BAPTISM

Baptism is the washing with water instituted by Christ, which is done in the name of the Father, and of the Son, and of the Holy Spirit, for the regeneration of eternal life, that is, the Father, Son, and Holy Spirit by this ceremony or eternal covenant are truly brought into agreement with the person baptized, that all the benefits of Christ belong to him, that he is of the people of God or true Church, that he is received into grace, that he is accounted righteous, that he is made a son and heir of eternal life, and that likewise the Holy Spirit is now given to him to begin the new motions of the new life in his heart, to work in him true fear, faith, and joy; and to put to death the desires of the old man, just as this ceremony itself depicts these double effects.

For the laving of water partly signifies the sprinkling of the blood of Christ, or the washing away of sins; and partly the putting to death of the old man. It also foreshadows the birth of the new man.

In the first place, therefore, the Anabaptists are to be condemned for excluding wretched infants from baptism, either because their sin is excused, as though they had no sin, or on account of the accusation of their reason, because they are not yet able to use it, and to believe. They are also to be condemned for repeating the ceremony, making any earlier baptism empty, and weakening the universal power of true baptism.

Secondly, just as the *hemerobaptistai*[17] once, because of their opinion that this covenant was made of no effect on account of subsequent sin, therefore used to repeat the ceremony (a great wickedness), so now the papists by their similar opinion and greater wickedness have substituted for the power of baptism their own works – not so much works of the divine Law, as works of human tradition – to the point that monks consider tonsure equal to baptism even among dead persons.

And as they impiously remove the use of baptism for the remission of sins after it is completed, so again they impiously posit another use, which baptism does not have from the Word of God:

---

17 That is – baptized for a day; transitory baptism; one which wears off.

namely, they say it is for the extenuation of the original sinfulness remaining in man's nature after baptism. Even that real efficacy itself, which is in baptism from the sole institution or ordination of God's will, they attribute directly to the water in a magical manner, some to the water on account of some secret hidden power, others on account of the assistance of the Word.

Finally, human recklessness has added its own filth to the essential things of baptism, namely, magical anointing: and by this devilish profanation they have transferred this sacrament to bells and stones. We also reject what the Adiaphorists have done: They defile this sacrament by the restoration of certain papistical ceremonies.

Concerning
the Lord's Supper

[handwritten: Lutheran overtoned]

Christ at the Last Supper instituted a covenant for His church, to wit, that His true body is to be eaten under the bread, and His blood to be drunk under the wine, as a perpetual ceremony until His last coming, so that by this consumption, each and every one might commemorate the Lord frequently in his life, that is, that he might awaken and strengthen his faith by this pledge, as it were, that the body of the Lord was handed over, and His blood truly poured out for the remission of even his own sins, and that he has truly been made, and is, a member of Christ and of the Church, and an heir of His goods; also, so that he may, by faith, incite a fuller affection toward the other members of the same body, or fellow heirs of faith; that he may proclaim and praise the Author of such great benefits, and that he may obey Him in all his life.

This covenant of our Lord Jesus Christ has been defiled by the Papists with their sacrilege:

1. By their mutilation of the institution, by which they have taken away part of the sacrament, namely the Cup, from most of the Church.

2. By their manifold and horrible profanation, in which they have diverted the sacrament to other, very different uses from the one which Christ instituted – nay, contrary to Christ and His merit – to wit, an offering not only for the living, but even for the dead; to merit *ex opere operato* remission of guilt and eternal punishment, both of purgatory and of this life; to secure goods corporal and spiritual. And they appoint particular Masses for these particular purposes. They also shut up the bread and carry it around as a spectacle and a piece of idolatry.

The Interimists are no better. They allow both parts of the Sacrament to the laity for a time, not because of Christ's institution, but because of their own dispensation, and with a plain condemnation of the entire use of this sacrament added. The application of the benefits of Christ and the action of grace, which Christ ordered to take place in our partaking, these men by their novel opinion ascribe to the sacrifice which happens in the Mass. And finally in the act of partaking or communion, they, along with the Papists, neglect faith and the straightforward use of the Sacrament.

Here we also condemn those who give in to the error of the Interimists and say that the Mass can be done at any time by a lone priest without any other communicants.

Last of all, we abhor the Zwinglians and their ilk, who deny, for whatever reason, that Christ is able to be, or is, partaken of in this Sacrament along with bread and wine according to His own word, truly, substantially, and in a bodily manner. Likewise we resist the Papists and Interimists who urge belief in the transubstantiation of bread and wine into the body and blood of Christ; and likewise the Adiaphorists, who restore the practice of elevating the elements in those places where it had previously been abolished on account of abuse or liberty, and who thereby also confirm the adoration of this Sacrament, especially since the Feast of Corpus Christi has been restored.

In the case of the Adiaphorists, we also condemn, along with these first opinions, the fact that they restore the Papistical Mass for the most part, and make the action of this sacrament different in both name and deed from communion. They thereby furnish an obvious opportunity for the restoration of all kinds of papistical abominations.

CONCERNING ABSOLUTION

Christ in the Gospel has not only given power to teach, but also power to apply remission of sins and the rest of His benefits through the Word, whether to many, or to individuals who seek it by faith. In the same way, on the other hand, He has also given power, not only to teach, but also actually to bring about a retaining of sins, of the wrath of God, and of damnation in the face of impious persons who do not repent. And each of these things – if the absolution, then also the retention of sins – which happen through His ministers (or through others in case of necessity), is efficacious in His place, not only before the Church, but even before God, from the institution and Word of Christ through the Holy Spirit, whom He has especially given for this efficacy and certainty, saying (John 20), "Receive the Holy Spirit etc." And so, he who receives absolution by faith, truly also receives remission of sins and the Holy Spirit, and the absolution is itself beneficial to stir up the faith of individuals.

To this absolution, which is an institution of Christ, confession, which was instituted by men, is powerfully helpful – not that absolution cannot happen without some enumeration of sins, or that it is of no benefit, but among other weighty reasons, that the sacraments should not be conferred upon the unexamined and unworthy, which is to the benefit of the consciences of both the ministers and those who partake.

Therefore, just as we condemn the abuse of absolution and confession among the papists, so in certain other men we rebuke the fact that they do away with – not only their use – but also the things themselves.

We also rebuke the Adiaphorists. When these men speak about absolution in their chapter on repentance, they say nothing about faith, and they add some general statements which, when they explain them, clearly indicate that they attach satisfaction for sins to absolution.

To these three Sacraments the papists and Interimists now add others, namely confirmation, ordination, matrimony, and extreme unction, and they claim that these others were equally instituted by Christ and are necessary for salvation. This is an obvious lie. Nor do they have any promise of the Gospel connected with these things, that pious persons should be able to apply the benefits of Christ to themselves with them and to exercise faith, which is the distinguishing feature common to the Sacraments handed down by Christ. Also, when the Adiaphorists fill up the number of popish sacraments with these things for the sake of the Interim, even though they may hold a different opinion about the ceremonies themselves, nevertheless since the Interim urges and sets up impious opinions together with the ceremonies, they also confirm the same things, albeit not without a great difference in doctrine and a certain distinction in many consciences.

OF THE CHURCH AND ITS MINISTERS, AND OF THE POWER OF THE CHURCH AND ITS MINISTERS,

CHAPTER 6

After the fall of our first parents, God immediately added the promise about Christ His Son, who was to be born of a woman in the fullness of time to terrify the head of the serpent. He did this so that through this added promise He might gather the Church back to Himself from among the human race. And God Himself always chooses, by His own will and decision, and shall hereafter continue to choose until the consummation of the world, a people and an assembly, sometimes greater, sometimes less, as a guardian of His promise. This people He also defends against the power of the Devil and secures ahead of time by the gift of the ministry of the Word and of the Sacraments. And this ministry is always effective by His own will and decision only in those persons out of the entire assembly who hear this Word and use these Sacraments. In them He kindles a true knowledge by the Holy Spirit; a trust in the promise that had already been given to the woman (namely, Christ), and likewise a true obedience; He forgives their sins; He declares them to be righteous, sons, and heirs of eternal life on account of Christ. And indeed only these persons, wherever they are scattered all over the globe, are the true Church or true people of God on the earth. Their number may be now greater, now smaller, but there is always some tiny assembly, brought together with the rest, and likewise hiding and invisible, having its own sins and errors in its members. And this invisible assembly is here and there mixed with another, much larger assembly, which has the ministry of the Word and sacraments, sometimes pure, sometimes less pure, from which arises the whole visible Church, in which there are many wicked persons. Of these, however, some are subsequently converted. From time to time, those who hold the tiller[18] are themselves enemies of the true Church. True members of this true Church, however, though they have the word and Sacraments in common with the rest of the multitude, yet shine forth beyond the rest like stars in their true obedience to God, and in persecution for their calling they build up their confession, and they suffer when they have to. By these things they are known, and the truly pious at length acknowledge them after their deaths.

So that we may speak about the Church of the New Testament, Christ gave to it the keys of the kingdom of heaven, just as He Himself received them from the Father. He did not give them to Peter or to the rest of the apostles only, or to their successors in the ministry, but first and principally He gave them to the whole visible Church, yet in such a way that the keys might most properly belong to the sanctifiers of the true Church. The Church later committed the administration of the keys to certain persons, for the sake of order only, by human judgment. As a result, the Church itself retains the whole right of the keys if its ministers, to whom they were entrusted, are unwilling to use them, or want to use them only for destruction. It also retains the administration of them in necessity, as when a supply of ministers cannot be provided in places where they are needed. But otherwise, it is not permissible for anyone to seize the ministry either publicly or privately without a legitimate calling by men.

Moreover, the power of the keys is the power to teach the Word of God, to administer the sacraments, to loose and bind the sins of individuals or groups of men, to call ministers, to hear and adjudicate questions of religion, to devise traditions that aid the ministry instituted by Christ – the keys bring with them the power to do all and each of these things, but in such a way that they all be done, not by human judgment and decision, but according to the command of the

---

18 Amsdorff compares the governance of the church to the steering (Lat. gubernare) of a ship.

Word of God, for the edification of the Church, not for its destruction, for the living only, and not for the dead.

Each one administers those parts of this power, and in those places, which the Church or those whom the Church has authorized, entrust to them, and as God has distributed a measure of His gift in each entrusted part. Hence there is this difference among ministers, by human ordination, according to which one minister oversees more churches than another, as a bishop or superintendent; and different officers take care of different parts of the ministry, as elders, pastors, councillors, and deacons. But for one man to take care of all these jobs in all the churches that require oversight in the whole world, or to become a universal bishop – since this is not handed down by the word of God, but is contrary to the Word, so it is impossible and destructive to the Church.

Although the gifts of ministers for carrying out their respective duties are different, and although ministers are often wicked and impious, nevertheless when they administer the substances of the Word and Sacraments, the worthiness of a minister does not increase the worthiness and efficacy of his ministry, nor does his unworthiness diminish it.

Against this summary and true exposition are ranged many detestable errors, of which we shall enumerate only these few:

The first error is that of the Donatists and Anabaptists, who, as though there were no visible church except of saints, order men to withdraw from the rest of the multitude which has a pure ministry, and institute their own assemblies, in which they say that all are equally saints.

The second error is that of the papists, by which they make the saints in the Church *anamartetous*[19], and necessarily associated together outwardly under one head, the Roman Pontiff.

Third, when the papists speak about the saints in the Church, they understand the dead to be nearly gods, to whom they command men to pray in blatant idolatry, and to seek help from them, to run to their statues and relics, etc.

Fourth, in their attempt to establish the primacy of the Pope of Rome there are many enormous errors. First, the fact that they

---

19 sinless

make him a universal Bishop over the Church of the whole earth by divine right. Second, they likewise by divine right ascribe to him alone the power of the keys, so that he receives it primarily, and others only secondarily through him. Third, they give him each of the two swords and full power over each of the two kingdoms, Ecclesiastical and Political. Fourth, they ascribe to him power and authority over the Scriptures, to change and manage everything concerning the Word, concerning the Sacraments and the commandments of God, to lay down articles of faith, to institute manners of worship and sacrifices, to change the nature of things, to bestow on them a new spiritual power for eternal life, to define questions of faith and morals, and above all, that he should not be able to err in all these things, and that it should not be right for any man to dispute or judge concerning his decrees and actions, even if he knowingly leads countless souls to hell.

Finally, they give him power not only over the living, but also over the dead, and over angels themselves. By these things it is now brought about that instead of the vicar of Christ, he is really the vicar of the Devil, and the Antichrist ruling in the temple of God, just as Daniel, Christ, and Paul have prophesied about him.

Lastly, the Adiaphorists abet these abominations in no small measure, when to the pope, whom they have earlier condemned from the word of God as the Antichrist, and whom they still condemn in their consciences, they grant the honor of primacy. And churches of Christ who have been happily freed from this evil creature, they by their adiaphoristical incantations, as it were, seize and force them under his tyrannical yoke.

The Adiaphorists are also to be rebuked for this: that in the Leipzig Decree they say that whatever the Church ordains ought to be taught, even though the Church ought not to institute any doctrine of religion, but only to hear what has been received from Christ. In this chapter it is obvious that they are equipping the council so that it may afterwards completely overturn the true religion for us.

OF POLITICS AND ECONOMY AND THE POWER OF EACH,

CHAPTER 7

Just as the Church is an ordinance of God, in which God wants there to be an order of teachers and of learners, so also politics and economy[20] are truly ordinances of God, in which He likewise wants there to be an order of superiors and an order of inferiors who are ruled by laws and precepts that agree with reason and are not at variance with the Word, and obey them, not only because of wrath or fear of the punishment which threatens from their rulers, but also because of conscience, that is, fear of the wrath and judgment of God.

For God has armed these His ordinances and powers with fear of both wrath and punishment, divine and human, and they both hold their respective power. And He has distinguished one power from another in His Word, so that He has attributed to each of them its own object and task, and likewise to each its own method of punishment. And although He does not desire the powers to be mixed up with each other, nonetheless He desires them to help each other in turn, so that in the end they all may agree, and that everything in its own place and way principally may promote the true knowledge of God and His Glory and their eternal salvation, or, when it does not attain this ultimate goal, may at least bring about a secondary sort of well-being, that men may live peacefully, uprightly, *kai ouk akarpoi*[21] in this civil manner of life.

Therefore polities and economies have been principally instituted, and are preserved and defended by God for the sake of the

---

20 By "politics" Amsdorff means the civil sphere. By "economy" he means not only economic life, but social life more broadly considered, especially the family.

21 not unfruitful

Church. Let those adults who are not continent all be joined together in marriage according to the word and commandment of God; let them become fathers and mothers of families; let them procreate; let them bring up the children and the rest of their families in the training and admonition of the Lord, as the Apostle says; that is, let them accustom themselves to honest work and true piety, and let them compel the disobedient with words and blows.

The legitimately called magistrate, from the word of God, ought to defend pious and honest citizens or subjects, and especially the Church, against injuries by the wicked, which he ought to prevent by bodily force and the sword; and with the greatest care he ought to see to it that men be taught rightly about religion, and that they conduct themselves publicly and privately for true piety and honesty.

In these matters, just as subjects necessarily owe obedience to their magistrates; and children and the rest of the family, to their parents and masters, on account of God; so on the other hand, when magistrates and parents themselves lead their charges away from true piety and uprightness, obedience is not owed to them from the word of God. Also, when they professedly persecute piety and uprightness, they remove themselves from the honor of magistrate and parents before God and their own consciences, and instead of being an ordinance of God they become an ordinance of the Devil, which can and ought to be resisted by His order for the sake of one's calling.

Moreover, since both political and economic life and authority are truly ordinances of God, therefore the Gospel not only approves of both, so that pious men may lawfully use them, but it even consecrates them, so that economic and political works, as a whole and singly, which are in agreement with laws and reason, and are not contrary to the word of God, are pleasing to God in believers, and become the worship of God.

Consequently, in the first place, this error of the Anabaptists is to be condemned: they deny that political and economic offices are permissible for Christians; they abolish magistrates, judgments, private property, contracts, etc., as though these things were evil in themselves.

The error of the papists is not much different from this one. *Prob*
They, although they do not indeed condemn political and economic
matters, nonetheless weaken them and treat them with notable contempt, while they deny that God is worshipped by these sorts of
life. Nay, they even forbid marriage to some men, i.e. to priests, contrary to the word and commandment of God. They do away with the
marriage contract or permit some priests to pretend to be married:
and this impure "celibacy" of theirs, with its abandonment of all the
common duties and risks of marriage, detestable for its laziness, lux-
ury, security and all impiety, they adorn with the title of "perfection"
in the spiritual sort of life.

Third, just as many consciences of good men are disturbed by
this weakening and distorting of political and economic offices
under the papacy, as they lightly esteem these ordinances of God,
and the majesty of political governors has been treated with contempt; so now, when the dignity of the civil and economic power
has been restored through the Gospel, some people are running
into sin in the opposite direction, so that they think that authorities are sacrosanct and inviolable even when they try to crush
the good work which they had a duty to honor; and when they
establish and honor on the other hand the evil work to which they
ought to have been a terror. We have taken this business up in the
following section of this book, where it will be discussed at greater
length.

EPILOGUE OF THE
CONFESSION OF DOCTRINE

Christian reader, you now have a summary of that doctrine which is founded on the prophetic and Apostolic scriptures, and which in these recent days has been again unfolded out of the great shadows of the reign of antichrist by the man of God, Luther of sacred memory – doctrine which was expressed in the articles of the Augsburg Confession, and still sounds, by the singular kindness of God, uncorrupted and pure in our churches.

If, in this exposition of the articles of true doctrine and then of dissenting opinions ancient and modern, we have said anything unsuitably or incompletely in our brevity, it may be cleared up for our hearers from our other meetings; but we desire the rest of the readers of this book of ours to think it better to drink more deeply from the writings of Luther, that great river laden with gold drawn from the sources themselves, or from the writings of other men like him. We will hope that nothing different from them is said in or received from this book.

We also have ceremonies in our churches which agree with the doctrine of the Apostles and the purer Church of the sub-apostolic age. These ceremonies are pious and useful for edification, just as we received them from churches outstanding for their true piety. And as we are able to change nothing from the doctrine of these Churches without grievous insult to Christ, dissent and blasphemy (nor do we want to, since Christ supplies our strength because we ask him and hope in him), so we judge that ceremonies are not able to be separated from doctrine by times and circumstances, nor are specious agreements between Belial and Christ – which some men are making, so that they may escape the cross – able to be allowed by that standard of judgment. This has been plainly shown in our previously published writings, and no one has so far been able to show otherwise. No one has dared so much as to touch the heart of this controversy by responding, which is the greatest evidence of a bad conscience in a wise and learned adversary.

Therefore we have now written this confession with our name and the name of our churches. The names of all men who are still openly pious and have not yet bowed their knees to Baal, who are with us in spirit, and whose prayers and groans are, we doubt not, joined with us. We have done this, first, so that we may render a witness of the truth to Christ who is now hanging on the cross; and so that we may present the necessary worship which He now urgently demands from all men; second, so that we may strengthen our brothers in Christ, wherever they are, by our opinion and example; and finally, so that we may free ourselves as well from suspicion of novelty or faction in true doctrine or true worship. We, who have been proscribed and made offscourings and shavings not only to our enemies, but even to our brothers, have no other aim in writing this book than that we may guard uncontaminated that sacred deposit of the man of God Dr. Martin Luther, in whom we consider ourselves blessed. And plainly we were blessed, and we boasted. But we also consider ourselves blessed today, and we boast in the cross of our Lord Jesus Christ. And in the end, whatever the event may be, we shall die with Christ, and we shall live with Christ, who helps us by His own Spirit, just as He has promised to give Him as a timely aid to those who ask in faith.

THE SECOND
PART OF THIS BOOK
CONCERNING RESISTANCE

If the Interimists and the Adiaphorists really are such as most of them desire to be considered, i.e. as those who retain the sincerity of their expounders of doctrine even against the papalists, then they now have no cause to ask us whether we have the same sincerity, since they also hear it from us now, and learn it from testimonies of things, i.e. from our synods and our public rituals. But if they accuse us of stubbornness for refusing to change the other things (I shall not now speak about the adiaphora themselves as they define them to be adiaphora, and which are becoming sins, denials, and apostasies), then with what face and with what conscience will they now condemn and oppose with weapons those ceremonies which they themselves earlier handed down to us as pious and useful, which they themselves preserved, and would still preserve, had they not been overcome by fear of danger? And so this part of our Confession and Defense shall surely lack no approval with that part of our enemies who are Interimists and Adiaphorists, but they will of their own will admit that we cannot be rightly condemned and opposed by Christians for our teachings and rituals.

With the other part of our enemies, who have always been Papists, although this claim is not simple, nor shall any evident proof, be it never so much, be able to free us from the accusation of heresy, nonetheless the majority of them, convicted by the light of the Word of God and the testimony of their own consciences, know that we are being wronged in this matter, and they have often admitted it in debates and other discussion. Certainly they all know, and ought to know, by divine law, natural law, and human law, even by their own agreements and promises, that we cannot be condemned and attacked when our case is as yet unheard. This case we have always brought forward to be heard by a true judgment.

But if any princes and states have cast off, along with the cause, the very right of the cause as well, anyone will easily understand that this prejudice neither ought nor can stand against any others, especially in a matter pertaining to the glory of God and the eternal salvation of all men, but that a few despised men should still rightly demand their right, even if the powerful and the Epicureans[22] should laugh at them.

But our enemies themselves are not able to recognize the foul repulsiveness and the towering injustice of their own actions. Therefore, so long as a certain righteous fear was also the author of this plan of theirs, they were diligent to hide their foulness with greater care, so that they might deny that the late war had been begun for the purpose of wiping out this religion before it could gain a legitimate hearing. Now, after their victory has been gained, they have control of affairs and have become fairly powerful, although they still pretend that there is some pretext of rebellion so that they may wipe out the poor remnants of this confession. Nonetheless they openly hold forth that the oppression of this religion is sought before its legitimate hearing in regions and states that have been surrendered. Our enemies have loaded these regions and states down with the greatest injustice and cruelty surpassing even that of the pagans. They have done this by their changes of religion, not only through the Interim, but even by the restoration of the entire popish system where and insofar as they are able.

Therefore – a thing which pertains to this part of our Defense – our magistracy has taken it upon itself to say something about this matter again: to wit, that this is the first and only cause of the outrages, proscription and death which we suffer. After the enemy had already tried to ruin our city, the Senate, after the abolition of impious doctrines and impious worship, took care to establish some Churches of its own with true doctrines and true worship, and then did the same also for the rest of the churches that had been

---

22 "Epicureans" is used here and elsewhere in Reformation Latin, as a general label for atheists.

abandoned by the papists. And now that the true doctrine and true worship has been abandoned, it does not want to receive false doctrines, idol-manias, and blasphemies. To prohibit these things, it also is taking the necessary steps for the defense of itself and its people.

I say that this is the first and only reason why the enemies are trying to destroy this city, and why the city in turn is taking necessary defensive measures. Even if no one has said it, it is nonetheless known among all who judge truly, so that not even the enemies themselves are afraid to admit it – they who first stepped forth as the actors of this tragedy – unless believing nothing but what one wants and what is pleasing to the belly is considered the highest wisdom of a certain Epicurean kind, though the judgment of one's own conscience and all one's senses fight against it. Nor do I think that there is anyone with even a middling knowledge of the condition of this city and its neighbors, and their public actions, who would not admit that it is necessary for us to seek nothing more in this war than peace and true religion, and that we are not swayed by the majesty or wealth of anyone.

But I leave the rest for our Senate and all good men to explain to competent judges what were the beginnings, what the progress, and what the result which the cause of our religion has had with our adversaries and with the chief magistrates, especially those who have truly joined with this confession.

It is now all the more needful that we should prove by our Defense whether a Christian magistrate can or ought to preserve his State and the Christian teachers and hearers in it against his own superior magistrate, and drive off by force one who is using force to compel people to reject the true doctrine and true worship of God, and to accept idolatry. ✷

In proving this hypothesis, we see that the true, and likewise the easiest method has been laid out for us, when we look at those in whose pages this is a question to be treated. Among them there are two orders of enemies, of whom we have already made mention above: there are the papists, and there are the Interimists with the Adiaphorists added to them. There is, however, a third order, of those who ought to make their defense, so that they may have a certain and firm comfort in the dangers of this defense.

49

Among these last two orders, there is clearly no need for this repetition of the question, especially because to most of them, by true arguments from the Word of God, and by natural knowledge of His Divinity impressed on the human mind, it has been clearly explained a little earlier – unless by chance the king's will and weapons have somehow changed the divine and natural right, and the demonstrations and rules of consequence, and even the entire laws of logic used in the assertion of this legitimate defense – just as they were able to do hitherto in many articles of Christian doctrine.

By the same sort of reasoning, twice 4 shall cease to be 8. Magistrates and subjects shall be bound by sure chains and mutual oaths, but it shall be permitted to magistrates, when they want, to be loosed and free from all obligation, while subjects shall always be bound in all circumstances and never be free. It shall be permitted to magistrates to exercise the utmost tyranny contrary to the laws and their oaths, but it shall not be permitted to the subjects to restrain the ravings of tyrants in accordance with the laws. Thus the truth of our common sense and the logic of consequences will always depend on the whims and weapons of those who have power.

Among our enemies the papists we have even proved, in vain, that defense against a superior magistrate who persecutes the true religion by arms is granted to an inferior magistrate, when they deny that this religion of ours is the true one, and deem that their war is therefore just – though they are not even right about that, as has been said above.

And so, in the mustering of this defense, we are especially motivated by the consciences of those who retain purity of doctrine, or those who do not want it to be overwhelmed and themselves to be persecuted, so that both sorts may know what they ought to do about this defense, and what comfort they have in it.

But first we call Charles Caesar (Charles V) to witness, our most merciful lord, that you not allow the popish forces so to abuse your majesty and power to expel, nay rather, to crucify Christ – Christ who, since He Himself has given you this most prosperous kingdom that you have, is now your guest in it, poor, rejected, and full of troubles in His members, i.e. His disciples, beseeching your faithfulness in the administration of the realm that has been entrusted to you, not seeking that any part of the kingdom or glory be returned to Him, but that defense or freedom from punishment be allowed, so that He may repay your faithfulness in these gifts with greater gifts in eternal life.

And if, stricken in your conscience, you are not yet able to consider us as disciples of Christ, we beseech you to think of your piety, that Christ, when he was handed over to be crucified by the chief priests among His people, was not considered as the son of God, but as a blasphemer and a seditious man. Likewise the Apostles and other martyrs were always so considered, and murdered by the usual authorities. Likewise, the Lord predicted this outcome in John 16: "They will put you out of the synagogues" and "the hour is coming when everyone who kills you will think that he is offering an act of worship to God."

In this utterance He also hands down the mark of the false church, i.e. that it will spread its religion with weapons. The true Church has never taught that men ought to be forced, even to true piety, by weapons. In the same manner, you yourself allow the Jews and pagans who obey your rule to follow their own religion; you do not force them with weapons to accept yours.

We poor wretches, since we are called Lutherans, are more unfortunate than these. Why have we been deprived of this kindness of yours? Together with you, with one mouth and one heart, we preach Christ, our shared redeemer and savior, and we embrace all the articles of the Christian faith. We are divided only in this, that to you who have been persuaded so by the papal party, we seem to ascribe to Christ too much of the merit and glory in justification, and because we judge that He ought to be worshipped only according to His own word, while you think that he also ought to be worshipped in more ways, and you force us to worship Him according to human traditions. See therefore, I beseech you, Caesar Augustus, how serious this matter will be for you in the last judgment of Christ, in which you will render an account to Him for all your deeds, and you will receive what your deeds have deserved. Consider what will happen to you if you, a Christian, are a persecutor of Christians, true members of Christ, because they seemed to you to extol Christ and His Word with excessive praise.

Sphere sovereignty

As for other matters relating to your rule, we will gladly render obedience – as much as we are able and we owe you. The profession of our religion has diminished nothing from it; so that much true dignity and encouragement for the obedience owed rather flows from it for you. For we teach with the apostle Paul that you are the vicarious minister of God for promoting good works, and that obedience is owed to you in this role, just as to God, not only because of wrath or fear of your sword, but also because of conscience, that is, fear of the wrath and judgment of God.

Although we cannot consider that all men equally comply with this doctrine, nor can we bring that about ourselves, nonetheless we can promise you this with the strength of a promise which is said about our ministry ("my word will not return to me void, Is. 55. Likewise, "Your labor will not be in vain in the Lord") that we will give from our Churches the greatest possible number of men who, if they be able to enjoy their own religion through you, will declare their obedience toward you in all owed and upright duties, and loyalty without hypocrisy, out of true love, not so much love of receiving fruit from you, as love of you yourself, perhaps more than all those whom you say are obedient to you, so that you mistakenly mark us for the crime of contumacy and rebellion.

Although we are not able to look into the hearts of individuals, still, let us plainly affirm this about the city's general attitude and will: that except for the preservation of our religion, nothing else is sought; that when this is gained, our Senate and citizens will be most obedient in all their proper duties according to your Majesty's laws. If the public's attitude and will did not seem altogether this way to us, rest assured that we would either force this whole Church to desist from what it has begun, by excommunication according to the command of Christ; or else, we would shake the dust off our feet and leave this city. We command them, by the word of Christ, to render unto God the things that are God's, and to Caesar, though he be different in religion, the things that are Caesar's. They render these duties of double obedience and conduct themselves without crime of their consciences on either side, and without rancor, when both sides keep themselves within the limits of their duty prescribed by God and by the laws. Again, when there is a departure on either side from these limits, then horrible sins and severe unrest cannot but arise. In this way now, you, Charles Caesar, are exceeding the limits of your dominion, and you are extending it into the dominion of Christ. Therefore you yourself are the cause of these disturbances, just as Elijah once said to Ahab. The cause is not those who are unwilling and unable, because of fear of the wrath of God and eternal punishment, to bestow on you honor that has been stolen from God.

All that is left for us to do is to entreat your Majesty Caesar Augustus, by the passion, cross, death, and resurrection of our Lord Jesus Christ, whose memory we celebrate together with you. By His most just and severe final judgment we urge you to cease at last from proscribing and persecuting us and other innocent Christians over a matter in which we are bound and obligated by Christ, your Lord and ours.

If we cannot obtain this from you – as so far we have not been able to obtain it, nor could others appointed as suppliants on our behalf – then you may be sure that you will hear a bad testimony from us before Christ the judge on the day of judgment, and our groans and those of other pious men will go up now against you in the sight of our God, and they will hasten your punishments. You also will force peaceful and righteous men to take up a necessary defense against your implacable and unjust savagery.

True though this opinion about defense is, we do not put it forth with any pleasure, especially because we think that many wicked men in the external society of the Church can seek to make this pious reason a pretext for some impious attempt of their own, and also that even good men are sometimes carnally impatient of injuries, and can badly abuse opinions that have been rightly handed down to them by employing them at the wrong time or place. For this very reason, we know that the greatest theologians before us were especially cautious, hesitant, and careful in setting forth this opinion, since it was not yet necessary nor beneficial for every curious inquirer to know it.

Now, however, your Ahitophels[23] especially desire to destroy us, and then to snuff out the entire Church of the pious who do not

---

23 Ahitophel was the traitor who tried to destroy David during Absalom's rebellion. (1 Samuel 15:12,31-34)

inwardly consent to idolatry. Their intent is plain to everyone. And to accomplish this enormous crime, they place their greatest hope, not less in your title than in your power, O Caesar. They wish to terrify everyone by this title as though by the lightning bolt of divine wrath, so that when no one resists out of fear of divine wrath, they may easily be able, through you, to restore the idolatrous abomination of desolation in the temple of God, or to kill all those who dissent, just as Antiochus once, at the time of the Maccabees, had no difficulty in cruelly slaughtering certain men who had been made unfit for war by a false scruple of conscience about violating the Sabbath, and entertained hope of destroying by the same way and means (on the Sabbath) the entire remainder of the people who clung to the commanded divine worship. He hoped to abolish the true worship of God, and by his will bring about uniformity of religion among all nations.

And so, since the same thing is clearly being moved by certain Antiochuses and Ahitophels of yours, whom you have in your court, therefore just as at that time Matathias, by freeing the consciences of the rest of the pious, armed them to fight against the king for their lives, as he himself said, and for the righteous ordinances[24] of their God, lest they perish from the earth, so we in our similar trouble and peril ought to free the consciences of our men from this vain bogey-man which is thrown up, that defense has not been granted by God against superiors; and we ought to encourage our people to be themselves imitators of the law, and to give their minds to the witness of our God, if perchance God may look on us with favor and give us some such outcome as He gave the Maccabees, as we hope and pray. But this doctrine which we hand down about the legitimate defense of a lower magistrate against a superior one who seeks the extirpation of the Gospel and the true Church — if the ignorant crowd should abuse it on occasion to the greater destruction or harm of our enemies, that is not a reason why that abuse should be imputed to the Gospel or to us. We would have desired even now

---

24 Righteous ordinances = Lat. *justificationibus*. Amsdorff clearly has in mind the New Testament epistles' use of the Greek *dikaiomata*, (Romans 2:26 and Hebrews 9:1, 9:10) but at the same time, he alludes to the centrality of the Lutheran doctrine of justification by faith alone.

to hide this true opinion as it had always been hidden hitherto, had we not been defeated by the present injustice and tyranny of certain men, and deemed that the preservation of the Gospel and the True Church ought to be put before such dangers from those ignorant men.

Therefore we again affirm from the sure Word of God that when superior magistrates attempt to force Papistical idolatry upon their citizens, to overwhelm the true worship of God and His true worshippers, just as they have now begun to do, by unjust maneuvers with their laws, even if they pretend otherwise – then pious magistrates are not only able, but even have an obligation to resist them as far as they are able, to defend the true doctrine, worship of God, life, modesty, and the property of their subjects, and preserve them against such great tyranny.

We will now rehearse the three clearest and firmest foundations of this opinion, omitting any further reasons.

THE FIRST ARGUMENT
FROM DEFINITION

The Magistrate is an ordinance of God for honor to good works, and a terror to evil works (Rom. 13). Therefore when he begins to be a terror to good works and honor to evil, there is no longer in him, because he does thus, the ordinance of God, but the ordinance of the devil. And he who resists such works, does not resist the ordinance of God, but the ordinance of the devil. But he who resists, it is necessary that he resist in his own station, as a matter of his calling. Next therefore it is the calling of another magistrate, either the superior or equal of him who inflicts the harm, or of the inferior who suffers the harm, who is himself the ordinance of God through the superior, to be an honor to good works and a terror to evil in his defense of his own citizens by the command of God. And as the superior is not able to alter this ordinance and command in respect to himself, so neither is he able to alter them in the case of another; nor is he able to give license to persecute good works and promote evil – no more than he is able to make the right of God and the right of Nature unrighteous.

When, moreover, he deposes an inferior magistrate who is unwilling to obey him in such a crime, and replaces him with someone who is willing,[25] by the very fact that he now honors and promotes evil works, and dishonors and destroys the good, he is no longer the ordinance of God, but the ordinance of the devil, and he makes this deposition of the good magistrate invalid before the judgment of God, and the deposed one remains still obligated to God to do the duty of a magistrate among his people – that is, to promote good works and reprove evil in whoever commits it, even his superior, just as Paul speaks indefinitely in that passage (Rom. 13), excepting no one, but treating the superior tyrant as an ordinance of the devil.

But if, of the inferior magistrates, the more important and the greatest number themselves also neglect to do their duty, they admit

---

25 Amsdorff is referring to Charles V deposing the Elector of Saxony, John Frederick, and replacing him with Maurice in order to carry out the Interim, and lay siege to Magdeburg.

a great crime by their negligence alone, nor does the example of those men either excuse the other magistrates (lesser and fewer) in the sight of God, or encumber them, that they should not be individually under an obligation to persevere in doing the office of a magistrate, each in his own place and way.

Here we must also distinguish different degrees of offense or injury. Since there is a great difference between them, we must consider whom a magistrate is able and ought to resist, and in what way, lest we suppose that we are permitted to make any injury we choose into an opportunity to disturb our superiors. First, then, as all men do, so especially magistrates by their natural weakness have their own vices and sins, by which, either knowingly or wantonly, they sometimes do injuries, not excessively atrocious, but remediable.

We do not at all wish inferior magistrates to exercise their own office against superiors with the sword in these cases, either to punish or to defend. They can also exercise their office by warning them seriously, and in other civil ways; indeed, they ought to. If they cannot avoid harm in this manner, let them bear the harms they can bear without sin, and by no means take up arms themselves.

1 Peter 2 properly pertains to this situation: "Let servants be subject to their masters with all fear, not only to the good and modest ones, but also to the ill-tempered, etc." Here we may also make a broader application of what is written in Exodus 22, "You shall not speak evil of a ruler of your people." And with that *epieikeia* or reverence with which Shem and Japheth treated their father Noah, so also let us all the rather cover the shames of our superior magistrates than expose them, even when they are joined with injuries.

The second level is that of atrocious and notorious injuries, as when a leader from a state, or Caesar from an individual leader wishes by unjust violence, contrary to his oath and the laws, to take away life, or spouse, or children, or privilege and sovereignty acquired by inheritance or law. In such a case, since we will say that no one is compelled by the command of *God* to submit to the usurpation of his own right, so neither will we say that anyone is terrified by the command of God, who himself also bears the office of a magistrate, that he should not use the authority of a magistrate in making the necessary defense. But we will hope that in this circumstance Christian magistrates are prepared to suffer even injuries of this sort, and to leave vengeance to God, when the injury affects individual men, or a few men; and when the injury is able to be tolerated without sin.

Here let us establish the third degree of injury to a magistrate, in which an inferior magistrate is so forced to certain sin, that he is not able to suffer it without sin if defense is omitted – for the sake of which he himself bears the sword, as when Pharaoh orders the midwives to kill the male children of the Hebrews, or if he were to order Moses to aid in the persecution of the Israelites. But here there is need for accurate and true judgment, lest in beating back injury, other higher laws be violated, which would make the repelling of the injury itself unjust too, and incite muttering. In these last two kinds, the magistrates who are the authors of such injuries properly become and are called tyrants.

The fourth and highest level of injury by superiors is more than tyrannical. It is when tyrants begin to be so mad that they persecute with guile and arms, not so much the just persons of inferior magistrates and their subjects, as their right itself, especially the right of anyone of the highest and most necessary rank; and that they persecute God, the author of right in persons, not by any sudden and momentary fury, but with a deliberate and persistent attempt to destroy good works for all posterity. If anyone advances in madness this way, even the highest Monarch who does so unwittingly, he is not merely a bear-wolf (to which Luther compares a tyrant in his disputation[26]), but is a very Devil himself, who is able to do nothing more wicked and great, except what he does with more knowledge, and this is the very essence, the formal cause,[27] of his holding office in the kingdom of the Devil.

And as the Devil, by this government of his, desires the extinction of the whole chain of knowledge of laws and divine promises, so in the whole human race he selects for himself suitable tools, of whom some serve the Devil in removing and corrupting some parts

---

26 In a 1539 debate, Luther compares the Pope and Holy Roman Emperor Charles V to a monster of German folklore, the Beerwolf.

27 Amsdorff alludes to the Four Causes found in Aristotelian philosophy: material, efficient, formal, and teleological ("final"). The formal cause of a penny is that it is a round coin with a picture of Abraham Lincoln on one side. Amsdorff means that persecuting the church is the distinguishing mark of an officer in Satan's kingdom.

of this knowledge; others, other parts. And he especially attempts to extinguish forthwith the chief and preeminent part of this knowledge, namely, the part that concerns the true worship of God and the salvation of the human race; and likewise to extinguish the true worshippers themselves, that is, the true Church of God. To this end he especially incites the chief magistrates, ecclesiastical and civil. As he did in the time of the prophets, Christ, and the apostles, so also in our day.

Therefore, if now the leader or Caesar proceeds to such a height of insanity only in that order of natural knowledge which governs the society of civil life and uprightness, that he abolishes the law concerning marriages and all chastity, and himself sets up a contrary law of roving unclean lusts, to the effect that the wives and daughters of all men are to be prostituted; and if he himself defends and prosecutes this law with force and arms, so that certain death is laid down as the penalty for those who resist or fail to conform – in such a case, doubtless, no clear-thinking person would have any hesitation about the divine right and commandment that such a leader or monarch ought to be curbed by everyone in his most wicked attempt, even by the lowest of the lowest magistrates with whatever power they have. Still less can anyone doubt, unless he is an atheist or an Epicurean or a Sadducee[28], that such resistance is also just and necessary in that highest level of Laws and divine knowledge that closely pertain to the glory of God and to the eternal salvation of each man, because both the glory of God among men, and the eternal salvation of each man cannot stand without them.

---

28 Amsdorff here uses both the Epicureans and the Sadducees as examples of wickedly sophisticated, this-worldly anti-supernaturalists.

The Epicureans were a sect of ancient Greek philosophers who taught a materialistic ontology in which all things are reducible to atoms and void. Though they acknowledged the existence of a deity, they were Deists, maintaining that god is so far removed from human cares and from this world that he cannot be troubled by the prayers or men, and does not intervene in history.

The Sadducees were a sect of ancient Judaism that denied the resurrection of the dead, "neither angel nor spirit" (Acts 23:8) Angel and spirit are here references to the interim state of the soul after death and before resurrection. The Pharisee party in Acts 23 was willing to allow that Paul might have seen Jesus' ghost, but the Sadducees could not accept such a notion, since they believed that death was the end.

This is being done by our highest magistrates. They are attempting to abolish by force the true knowledge of God among us and all men for all posterity. Without this knowledge God cannot be truly worshipped, nor can any mortal be saved. They desire to justify false and blasphemous opinions about God and to plant them in the hearts of all men, and to establish the sole rule of Antichrist and of the devil against Christ. Since they do these things, it is clearer than the light of noon, so that it can be plain even to those who doubt the response which certain men have received from the prestigious emissary: that Caesar is not able, without committing perjury, to exempt anyone from anything of the common decree of the Imperial states which was enacted at Augsburg in the Interim. From this response, as well as from many other testimonies and outcomes of affairs, one can well reckon what may be expected hereafter not only for us, but also for all others who persevere in true piety. This is the chief cause of our proscription and the reason why we did not make a reconciliation with Caesar. Whoever is able, or wants to, may figure it out.

Finally, whoever is pious and sound of mind should reckon from this whole exposition what, in the present business and danger, befits us and all pious men, whether lowly persons or magistrates; likewise what befits those on both sides who are called to military service: what, whom, and with what conscience and expectation of divine judgment they are fighting, or shall fight in the future.

Since this first Argument was taken up from the manifest word of God, from the immutable principles of nature and from the witness of events, so it is especially true and unshakeable in this debate. It furnishes an illustrated spectacle of an incalculably horrendous crime among our enemies, while among those who are making this defense it commends not only their justice, but zeal as well. It promises eternal rewards, with a worthy outcome for those who are zealous for the law of our God.

THE SECOND ARGUMENT

When Christ commands, with an affirmative and by clear inference, that the things which are Caesar's are to be rendered unto Caesar, and the things which are God's to be rendered unto God, we rightly infer from the affirmative a negative, likewise by clear inference, just as negative commandments, as in the Decalogue, always include an affirmative sentence by direct inference. And so by the force of this precept, the things which are God's are not to be rendered unto Caesar, just as the Apostles hand down this rule and precept, "We must obey God rather than men." And by refusing obedience to superiors in those things which are contrary to God, they do not violate the majesty of their superiors, nor can they be judged obstinate or rebellious, as Daniel says, "I have committed no crime against you, O king." For two reasons free them from this charge: First, because those who wield the magistracy do not demand this obedience as magistrates by the ordinance of God, but as men, that is, having no superiority from the word of God. The apostles appear to have wanted to judge this case by their own dictum. Then, even if they remained true magistrates, even still, as in human ranks the law of the superior power trumps the law of the inferior, so divine laws necessarily trump human ones.

Secondly, as Christ does not want the things of God to be ascribed to Caesar, so He does not want to see any things ascribed to him [Caesar] that are others' and not his, whether according to divine laws or even the laws of his own empire. If, contrary to these laws, Caesar should demand my life or some other man's life, or the chastity of a wife or daughter, or property etc., I ought not to allow them to him. Thus there was no price whatsoever at which Naboth was willing to sell his vineyard to his king Ahab (1 Kings 21). Ambrose was not willing to allow his sanctuary to the Arians and the command of the Empress Justina. Lawrence was not willing to hand over the treasure of the Church to Decius[29]. Would that leaders as well as subjects were thinking of this right and these examples!

---

29 Lawrence was the archdeacon of Sixtus the bishop of Rome. He was besieged and brutally martyred by Roman Emperor Decius for giving the Church treasures to the poor,

Third, just as Christ by clear inference orders the things of Caesar to be rendered unto Caesar; and to God the things which are God's, and likewise to all men the things that are theirs, so when Caesar demands what is his, or what is owed to him, so that he may snatch things that are necessarily bound up with it that belong to God or others, and they cannot be given him without sin, then the clear inference orders us also to deprive Caesar of the things which are his or which are owed to him.

Let us take an example concerning a father of a family. If he should come to his wife or grown daughters in his house with some scoundrels in an obvious attempt to prostitute them, then they, his wife and daughters, not only would not render their husband and father the obedience which they otherwise owe him, but when they are not able to preserve their chastity in any other way, they would drive him off with stones.

By the same argument, when the admission of Caesar into a magistrate's city brings with it a sure abolition of the true religion, the slaughter and exile of pious men – in this case, the defense of religion, of one's own life and the lives of other innocent persons (which defense the magistrate of that city owes to God and to the citizens by the commandment of God) removes another part of the obedience owed to Caesar, that he should not offer obedience by admitting Caesar into the city, according to the rule of Christ, because the duties owed, when they come with injury to God and others, and joined with sin, ought not to be paid to anyone, not even to a father or a magistrate.

Fourth, Christ by this same sentence ("Render unto Caesar the things which are Caesar's, and to God the things that are God's), as He subjects other men to Caesar, so he also subjects both them and Caesar himself to God, and He wishes the greatest power among men, as is the power of Caesar, to be especially subservient to God, by taking care that just as Caesar himself, so also the rest of the subjects under his power, should render to God the things that are God's according to His word, and should restrain those who do otherwise(That this is the proper and principal job of a Christian magistrate, and especially of that highest

---

rather than allow them to be seized by the State.

Prince, is here roughly indicated, but is proved more clearly in other ways by our testimonies, arguments and examples from the word of God.

Therefore, when the highest prince himself not only does not render to God the things that are God's, but also snatches divine honor from others on the pretext of his power, and claims it for himself by the sword, then there nonetheless remains among men this very power ordained by God, to vindicate the honor of God. And as when Caesar is dead, the rest of the princes and states under him will all use, in their own places, as much of Caesar's power as has been transferred to them; and because of the commandment of God, they ought to use it to prohibit blasphemous men, and those who use the sword to force others to blaspheme; and they ought to drive them off from their own necks with the sword – so now, by the same power, they ought to prohibit the highest prince himself from doing the same things beyond and against his own office – doing them, I say, by the ordinance of the devil, not of God, as has been shown from Paul above. What is said in the Psalm is also relevant here: "I have said, 'You are gods,' yet you will die like men" – that is, "When you abandon My ordinance, by which I have set you over other men to bear my authority among them by honoring good works and punishing evil, and devote yourselves to shameful acts, just like the rest of evil men, then, because you have no grounds for your majesty and power, you will be punished just as they are, by Myself and by others, to whom I have given this power, each in his own place, to punish and restrain evil men.

THE THIRD ARGUMENT

I f God wanted superior magistrates who have become tyrants to be inviolable because of his ordinance and commandment, how many impious and absurd things would follow from this? Chiefly it would follow that God, by his own ordinance and command, is strengthening, nay, honoring and abetting evil works, and is hindering, nay, destroying good works; that there are contraries in the nature of God Himself, and in this ordinance by which He has instituted the magistrate; that God is no less against his own ordinance than he is for the human race.

All these things are most plain, nor can they be denied by anyone: If God has granted such great impunity to the greatest tyrant by His own ordinance and commandment, who will prevent him from laying waste all of nature, even if he could, and being innocent before God? Who will not provide his substance, his body, and even his life itself to the one who demands them for the occasions, ends, and nourishment of tyranny, because of the commandment of God? Who will do what is right contrary to the will of a tyrant, and be a survivor? Who will be left of all men as the only one doing right? Therefore God wants, and does not want, evil; he destroys and builds up evil by his own ordinance in magistrates. And since nothing is more familiar and easy for men than to abuse for evil the power and impunity granted by God for good; nothing easier for the Devil than to incite such a man, and make a devil out of the man; and since nothing can be more hoped-for by the devil, and more suited to establish his reign (which is the reign of sin and death) than to constrain the consciences of men by the certain word and commandment of God, so that they may not dare to stop him from doing his business through a magistrate ordained by God – from all these things, it is manifestly obvious that when the highest prince has been driven into madness, God, by his own ordinance and commandment, has overturned what is good in the ordinance of a magistrate, and has more truly betrayed His own laws than promoted them[30]; and has exposed righteous men to the fury of a tyrant and of

---

30 The Latin contains a pun: "verius prodidisse quam promovisse."

the devil. And so, just as everyone ought to hate the voice that Satan uses to prattle on about the power of the Roman Pontiff – that he has such impunity that even if he should knowingly lead countless souls to hell, nonetheless no one would be able to say to him, "What are you doing?" or to resist him (and indeed, by this horrible lie Satan has established the tyranny of the Antichrist beyond measure) – so now we also understand from true causes that that persuasion about the impunity of the highest prince, or of superiors, is not only empty, but is an invention of the devil, designed at this time especially to destroy the remnants of the kingdom of Christ, and to restore the kingdom of the Antichrist and of Satan himself.

Nor is it any objection to our reasoning that God Himself has both suppressed, and is still able to suppress, tyrannical persecutors of the Gospel and of the Church; and that the kingdom of Christ is neither established by the sword, nor has any need to be defended and preserved by the sword.

God has always punished wicked men, and especially tyrants, partly without the ministry of men, by His own various means, some secret, others open; and partly through the instrumentality of men. Again, sometimes He punishes the wicked themselves by means of the wicked; but ordinarily He does so through those who are called to exercise just punishment, according to what is said about homicides: "Whoso sheds man's blood, by man shall his blood be shed" (Gen. 9).

This means of carrying out punishment and driving off unjust violence is divine and belongs to magistrates, whether to the superior against the inferior, or to an equal against an equal, or to an inferior against a superior. For God has shared[31] this His own honor with all legitimate magistrates, not with only one rank or one person. He has given it for the defense and honor of good, not of evil works, for the whole extent of this life, not in only one place or another, just as Paul speaks in a general way in his definition of the magistrate, excepting no rank or person or evil or time when good men should not be defended by the office of any magistrate, even the lowest. Or if there *is* an exception for superiors and their sins, by which they seek to snuff out right and religion, it will be necessary to deduce

---

31 Literally, "communicated" in the theological sense, *e.g. communicatio idiomatum.*

this exception from the explicit word of God. But no one has ever shown it to us. Rather, we can more fully demonstrate that God is not a respecter of persons[32] that he should sanction impunity by His own word and ordinance, especially of the highest crimes, but rather by this very ordinance of magistrates He most severely prohibits respect of persons in the distribution of punishments: For He says to Moses and Joshaphat[33], "The judgment which you render is God's". Therefore when a magistrate suppresses a tyrant, it is apparent that the same is suppressed by God.

What an absurdity it would be for God to have thus made the ordinance of a magistrate so holy and necessary for the human race, if one man should be in possession of it, and should be able to ruin nearly everything by his own will when he is driven into a frenzy, or to turn magistracy into its opposite, but if the rest of men are able, or wish to preserve that ordinance by a certain order without confusion, they should not be allowed to by God?

Last, we respond very simply and truly concerning the establishing and defending of the kingdom of Christ, that it indeed cannot be brought about by counsels or arms or other human means, but nonetheless, just as the work of a pious magistrate, by the ordinance and commandment of God, can and ought to serve the kingdom of Christ by instituting and honoring the true ministry of the word and sacraments, so also a pious magistrate's arms ought to serve the kingdom of Christ in the same ministry by defending the whole Church against unjust persecution.

These are very strong arguments to prove the necessary defense of an inferior magistrate against a superior in the present persecution of the gospel. They are also sufficiently powerful to educate the consciences of all pious and good men so that they may know, all and each, the obligations of those who are ordered to train their weapons against the gospel of Christ, or to beat back those weapons.

The remaining arguments for this opinion, and likewise those which are contained in Roman law, are known from the writings of the chiefest theologians before our day, and those of others who

---

32 Amsdorff uses the Greek *prosopoleptor*, but I have replaced it with a translation.

33 That is, Jehoshaphat, the son of Asa. The very name means "YHWH has judged" in Hebrew. (2 Chronicles 19:4-7)

agreed with us in the assertion of this defense before this persecution arose against us. And we are not changing anything in this opinion, nor are we saying anything new, just as we do not change anything in the other articles of the pure doctrine. And the same opinion may be found from Luther the man of God, since it was set forth in some letters and other writings, and then also defended in a public disputation long before the start of the war. But as to why the same Luther has often disputed ambiguously in certain other writings about this same subject, he himself has explained the reason for his counsel to some men in private, and he indicates it publicly enough in the book he published against that sly fox of Dresden[34]: He says that he wanted to restrain both sides: He did not want to say that defense was entirely illicit, lest he thereby give weapons to the papists; but he also did not want, by praising and approving of defense, to make good men remiss about tolerating the not too severe injuries inflicted by their enemies, and instead stir up all the more certain crazy Thrasones[35], whom he knew to be stupidly desiring war for quite other reasons, out of carnal desires. He complains most severely about those men in his commentary on Psalm 118. We also would prefer to do likewise, if affairs were still, as then, in one piece. But now, since there are scarcely even small remains of the pious left, and to consume them the papists are equipping with a sort of devilish contempt of Christ and His word such men as have now departed from us contrary to their own conscience; nor do they desire so much to see the wretched destroyed who remain, as to see the doctrine and glory of Christ destroyed in them, and the abominations of Antichrist established for all posterity – since all this is so, we are now surely compelled by the manifest exposition of the true opinion about defense, to place this most certain overthrow of Christ, the Gospel, and the Church, not only

---

34 Probably Amsdorff means either George the Bearded, Duke of Saxony, who made strenuous efforts to suppress Lutheranism in his dominions until his death in 1539, or else the prebend of Dresden, Jerome Emser, with whom he had some exchanges of views. Luther wrote a tract entitled *Against the Assassin of Dresden* to refute slanders by Duke George, so that he may be the more likely candidate. Also, Luther's usual insulting epithet for Emser was not "sly fox" but "the Leipzig goat," since Emser's family crest depicted that animal.

35 Thraso was a boastful and rich soldier in Terence's *Eunuch,* a Roman comedy whose stock characters became by-words for character traits among Renaissance and Reformation writers.

ahead of the punishments threatened by our persecutors, but even far ahead of the entire world.

Last, if anyone requests examples of this sort of defense by inferiors against superiors, he will find plenty and suitable ones enough, if he makes a summary of the deeds recorded in sacred histories, ecclesiastical and pagan.

The deeds of the Maccabees are nicely fitting in this connection. Since they were conquered and at that time under the Empire of king Antiochus, nonetheless since he desired to make a single common religion among all the nations, and was forcing the people of God to the worship of idols, they resisted him and defended both their own lives as well as the Law or worship of God, as it is expressly written there (1 Maccabees 2).

Jehu, one of the military leaders of king Joram, took up arms against his own king in order to bring about punishment for him and for the whole house of Ahab, because of the persecution of the true worship and the pious people that they had committed (2 Kings 9). And though he did this by a special calling of God, and also did certain unique things, nonetheless God wanted to illustrate by this example the general calling of pious magistrates, by which they ought to resist their superiors who persecute the true worship and the true Church.

The people of God freed Jonathan the son of Saul from his father's hand with a severe rebuke, when he was superstitiously wanting to kill him, and they either defended him by force, or certain were ready to defend him by force, and that not without just reason (1 Samuel 14). For they said, "As the Lord lives, not a hair from his head shall fall to the ground, since he worked with God today."[36]

Also the example of Asa who removed his mother from office and abolished her idols, when we think on it carefully, brings no small degree of light and weight to this debate (1 Kings 15).

Similarly also the example of Ambrose who by his anathema drove away Theodosius from the entrance of the church because of

---

36 Amsdorff quotes the Vulgate rendering of 1 Samuel 14, which translates the Hebrew oath formula literally. The form is elliptical: "As YHWH lives, [May some self-malediction be brought to pass against me] if a hair shall fall from his head..." The same elliptical conditional oath may be found in Hebrews 3:11, which is literally, "If they shall enter my rest," but is usually rendered, "They shall never enter my rest" by most English translations, who do not preserve the Jewish oath-form.

the slaughter of the Thessalonikans which he had committed (Trip. Hist. lib. 9).

The Armenians, when they had become Christians, defended themselves by arms against the edicts of the Emperor Maximinus who was forcing them to exchange the Christian religion for the worship of idols. And the Emperor Constantine took up arms for the defense of Christians against Licinius his co-emperor (Eusebius, *Church History*, lib. 9).

The most praiseworthy and powerful emperor Trajan, out of the innermost sources of natural law, pronounces on this question of defense by inferiors against superiors in political affairs. When he appointed a Master of the Horse for himself, he handed a sword to him, saying, "Use this sword against my enemies, if I give righteous commands; but if I give unrighteous commands, use it against me." This saying is celebrated and is truly of the law of the nature, that is, of divine law. Therefore, just as Christ in the gospel does not abolish the knowledge of theoretical or practical principles, or the Law of God itself, but rather establishes it, as the Apostle says, so neither does He abolish this opinion concerning necessary defense, but rather, Christian magistrates may piously use it – nay, they are under obligation to do so, because of the commandment of God, as we have already demonstrated at length by testimonies, arguments, and examples from the Word of God.

If anyone thinks we have been too harsh in explaining these things, let him consider that Christ suffers much harsher things in this persecution, and He demands that we testify to the truth, in saying which we have tempered our style not a little, so that a wise and fair reader may easily notice that we only wished to speak about the things themselves, and to spare persons as much as could possibly be done. If we do not attain peace, we are able to sharpen the things which have been said here, and we can add many others which tell heavily for our duty, even if the same reward awaits us in this world as the Prophets, the Baptist, Christ, the Apostles, and many others like them received for their similar work.

THE THIRD
PART OF THIS BOOK
THE EXHORTATION

Although a wise reader, from the things we have mentioned above in the confession and apology, easily understands, not what we are urging, but what God requires from each person, whether from those who are outside, or from all of us in this city and Church; as well as how men on the two respective sides can and ought to be afraid of bringing unjust violence upon us, and to be comforted in the driving off of the same – nonetheless, so that these duties and the reasons for them may be more in view, we have briefly composed certain special remarks as a sort of epilogue.

First, it is obvious that no pious or Christian person can bring aid to our enemies either by military means, or by giving plans, money or other things by which our enemies are armed. The only reason why our city is not able to attain peace is the fact that the Gospel is always stipulated in the terms of peace, and we are not free to change or diminish anything from it; and the enemies manifestly present that they are seeking the suppression of this whole doctrine of Christ, and the restoration of the Antichrist by every means at their disposal. How then, I ask, can anyone deny that we are not being attacked in this war primarily on account of political reasons, about which our people would easily agree, but that Christ himself is principally attacked, and His word, which we do not want to lose, or to receive the abominations of the Antichrist?

Therefore, whether you be a magistrate or a subject in any way involved in this war or in the carrying out of proscription, consider to what you are lending your counsel, money, work, body, and even your very life and soul; and to what allies. Is it not to the enemies of Christ and His word? And is it not to this very work, by which they desire to exterminate the knowledge and glory of Christ, not only from their own territories, but even from the whole world, and to replace them with papistic idol-fanaticism and blasphemies? With what Satanic madness do they persecute Christ in His members, and pollute their hands with the blood of Christ, and trample Him with their feet!

Nor will anyone be excused in the judgment of God because he does not know that this is being done, just as many of those who crucified Christ did not know that He was the son of God, and were not for that reason excused. For they ought to have known it from the speeches and miracles of Christ, just as all men now ought to know the public actions that relate to the glory of Christ and His health. And so that these actions may be better known, we are now making them public to all. If anyone hereafter is still ignorant, he will be ignorant and he will be ignored, for they are willfully ignorant of a thing obvious and explained to everyone.

And as affected ignorance does not at all excuse these men, but they are nonetheless persecutors of Christ, so much less will others be able to claim their will as an excuse, although it was coerced. It is nonetheless their will, and therefore, even more than ignorance, it shall bear the reward fitting to persecutors. And this is now the appearance of things with most people who hitherto have professed the gospel of Christ together with us: if anyone powerful were able to hand Christ over to be killed again in the flesh when there are set before him punishments or death, life or rewards of honor and wealth, he would have many Christians obeying his word – of whom, some would be caught by the sweetness of this present life, by rewards and honors; others, overcome by other means, so long as they also see Christ the Son of God placed in a position of weakness and abandoned by God – and they would crucify Him again to the will of the tyrant.

Hence it now arises that we are less surprised at the malice and savagery of the Jews against Christ in everything that was done in His passion and death, since we now see, with the greatest grief, similar persons and actions among many disciples of the Gospel (such as some were hitherto, or want to seem). And we will shortly see this even more.

Among the apostles, there are not only men grieving, muttering, fleeing and denying at the crucifixion of the Lord, but there are also men like Judas. There are among the others those who suddenly change the glad acclamation "Hosanna" on Palm Sunday into the fatal and cruel shout of "Take Him away, take Him away, crucify Him, crucify Him": There are men laying on schemes, taunts, hands, whips, plundering, and all the very things that precede the crucifixion itself.

Hence arises this sudden metamorphosis of the disciples of the Gospel: It is doubtless the fruit of their departure from the Word. This departure is first made in their heads, against their conscience, and soon creeps into their other members.

For when our leaders and states in the recent Augsburg convention,[37] abandoning the Word, in their first council, promise that they and their people will obey the Interim, and now without penitence certain men are seeking excuses, escape, even pretexts for impiety, while Caesar, withdrawing the pledge he gave, commands us to be harassed by a certain law of his, and will soon command all others as well to be harassed and massacred who do not acquiesce in the entire Interim or Papacy. And here, since perhaps few or none will be willing to retract their impious promises, or be willing to suffer anything themselves, they knowingly become crucifiers of Christ Himself in the persons of all the pious. Thus this impiety has its horrible growth, when men knowingly depart from the Word in their doctrine.

But an even greater punishment is security, by which most men are able to treat so great a crime with contempt – nay, even to excuse it, praise it, and boast about its wickedness. And this security is the first penalty of sin against the Holy Spirit in those who, to their rejection of acknowledged truth, are now adding persecution, since this sin is certainly being committed by many at this time. As for the fact that Christ says this sin is unforgivable, that does not mean that it cannot be forgiven for those who repent, but that such persons

---

37 The 1548 Diet of Augsburg, at which Charles V established the Augsburg Interim.

never do repent, being abandoned by God, so that this passage of the Psalm applies to them: "He has loved cursing and it will come upon him; he did not want blessing, and it will be far removed from him." Hence they become either open despisers of God, or, when they feel the wrath of God they soon despair, as Cain and Judas did. Our present times will shortly give many awful examples of this sort of men. If any men, with Peter, knowingly deny [sc. Christ] by way of weakness, or unknowingly persecute Him with Paul, we pray for them, that God may grant them repentance like that of Peter and Paul.

But we warn individuals not to trust in this distinction between persecutors; for those who knowingly persecute the acknowledged truth are committing a sin against the Holy Spirit, and no one of them has ever returned to penitence, according to the word of Christ. And how many of the others, who have unknowingly persecuted, are said to have been converted?

And I do not even know which of the two is a greater crime, to not know that the doctrine which you are persecuting is true, as Paul did not know, when he was persecuting Christians; or to unwittingly persecute, along with open persecutors, that which you yourself hold for the doctrine of Christ. However much Caesar now says that he is not persecuting us on account of our doctrine, but on account of our rebellion or other sins, nonetheless all who are serving in his military from among Evangelicals cannot but know that Caesar is at the same time especially persecuting this religion among us, and that the rebellion of which he accuses us arose because of the need to defend that religion. And so those Pseudo-evangelicals who aid Caesar against us by counsel, vows, money, or arms, are, after all, persecutors of the acknowledged truth, whether or not they know that they are committing such a crime; and whether they want to know or not.

And those who die in this run-up to war, or who shall die later in the actual conflicts, shall they not die as persecutors of Christ? How then will they be able to hope for forgiveness from Him whom they are persecuting, or to excuse their deed or deny that they have persecuted Christ in this war, since conscience itself then will rightly warn them? – conscience, which does not suffer dissimulation and darkness at such a time, but stands according to the truth of what has been done, bare and alone before the judgment of God.

But to be sure it is a great testimony of the wrath of God, both of His imminent righteous judgment, and of the last spasm of the Devil against Christ, that Christian men are now impelled to persecute their own true religion with weapons which pagan men hesitate to use or pick up to preserve their false religion. All the histories of all other times, ecclesiastical as well as pagan histories, can show nothing like it since the beginning of the world.

Hence this sin will afford the most horrible spectacle of all to God, to angels, to men, and to all of creation in the final judgment of God. It will also bear the most atrocious penalties of all with the devils. If it is revealed to anyone in their conscience even in the time of this life, that God will doubtless display the signs and examples of His judgment in them, then they will have the same comfort and reward as Judas did, and they will hasten to receive the worthy reward for their deeds in eternal death.

Although these things are spoken of in a horrible way, nonetheless they have not been spoken of – nor can they be spoken or thought by anyone – in such a way as to equal the magnitude of the sin and the divine wrath. Nor do we set these things forth to the world only out of an excessive anxiety to save our own life, since we acknowledge our weakness. Rather, overcoming the flesh by faith, we are firmly convinced that by this very loss of this life, we can carry off glory and the crown of martyrdom. But therefore we put forth our case all the more urgently, because we are under obligation to fight on behalf of the gospel of Jesus Christ against Satan and his ministers. We must do this not only by refuting his lies, but also by hindering his slaughters, whenever he fiercely attacks true piety by either of these means. Finally, we ought to have a very great motive in our little children, and all our descendants, for if we here, and other pious people elsewhere, are all slaughtered by Satan and the impious world, it will be no small hindrance to their eternal salvation.

Let the wise men and Epicureans mock these things, so long as they will also mourn later. Let the tyrants rave all the more, that they may fill up their measure the more quickly, and that we may now see this, even if by God's will we ourselves cannot be rescued, so that by our forewarnings we may save other good men who can be saved outside our city, and so that we may leave the seed of the Word to our posterity for eternal life.

And now we address those brothers of ours in Christ Jesus, who we do not doubt are very many in all churches, even those oppressed by tyranny, who should not want the purity of the Evangelical doctrine to be overwhelmed, and papistic idolatries to be restored. Still less should they want to become persecutors of the gospel and Christ themselves, or abettors and defenders of Antichrist, and to load themselves down with the sins of the whole kingdom of the Antichrist. Nor should they want to disturb this library-workshop[38] which Christ has instituted here for the whole Church in this hour of the power of darkness, to oppose the Antichrist by His weapons, namely the spirit of His mouth, etc.

That those who are of this sort may piously consider these things in their minds, it is necessary for them also to think that now is the time when they ought to confess Christ by their mouth and by their deeds; now, when they are able to confess him, though not without certain perils. For no one is so wise at this time, in my judgement, that he can escape all dangers and evils without certain denial or persecution of Christ. As for those who do not believe this, let them enjoy their slumbers now. In a little while, that small and brief loss which they did not want to suffer in their bodies or their property, let them bear it much more seriously in their consciences and minds (may it not be eternally!). There are many now with us and in other places who bear witness with both their voice and their writings to the unrest of their own consciences, which they have willingly inflicted on themselves at the beginning of these upheavals – some by timidity, others by cleverness, others by spurious excuses for their consciences.

In the life of Maurice[39] we have a record of the Theban legion. When the Emperors Diocletian and Maximian, most hostile to

---

38 Amsdorff means his publishing operation, by which he produces his tracts.

39 This entire paragraph is a retelling of the legend of St. Maurice (Mauritius) and the Christian legion from Egyptian Thebes, found in a letter of Eucherius, bishop of Lyon (c. 434–450). Maximian is said to have first ordered the recalcitrant legion decimated (i.e. every tenth man to be executed), then decimated again. When they still refused to kill their fellow Christians, he ordered the execution of the entire 6,666-man legion.

Christians, ordered the Thebans themselves to take up their weapons to subdue rebels against the Roman Empire. In accordance with the command of Christ, which orders us to render to God the things that are God's, and to Caesar the things that are Caesars, the Thebans, since they were still uncertain against which rebels the war was being readied, sent a certain chosen legion of soldiers to the Emperor, but with this command, that they should aid the Emperor in righteous wars, but should not stir their weapons against Christians, but rather should defend them against unrighteous violence. Maurice was designated as the leader of this legion.

So Maurice came with his legion to the Emperor Maximian, and when his whole army had been gathered at Ortodorum, he received his orders, that at the beginning everyone should swear hostility by oath against the rebels against the Roman Empire, and especially Christians, whom (just as is happening now to us) the Emperor judged rebels only because they refused to cast away their faith in Christ and make sacrifices to idols.

Then Maurice and all the pious soldiers separated themselves and reported to the Emperor that they were not doing anything seditious, and that they were indeed the Emperor's soldiers, and ready to defend the Republic with their arms, but that they would not depart one inch from the faith of Christ or do anything against Him. And those brave soldiers of Christ stood so firm in this most holy assertion that those who were not able to escape the hands of the whole rest of the invading army all undertook martyrdom themselves with a submissive will rather than attack others or deny their Lord and the Author of their life and salvation.

The followers of King Saul by their highest consensus and unity did not follow the command of the king to kill the priests of Nob, and thus they brought upon themselves the hatred of the king and the dangers that followed with it. (1 Samuel 22) If there were a similar consensus and unity of many good men now – which there certainly ought to be, from the commandment of God – about refusing troops, supplies, and contributions for oppressing us and other pious men, then even if those Sauls still had their Idumean Doegs, still the pious themselves would first have found some cure for their own consciences in this fact, that many men together are not easily forced to commit so great an injustice, and thus perhaps they might have escaped without punishment like the followers of Saul. If they were not able to escape without punishment, they might rather flee or suffer or even employ the defense of inferior magistrates that is granted against unjust violence by divine law (as has been demonstrated above) as well as by natural and human law, and especially by the prerogative of our German Empire, according to which superiors and inferiors are mutually bound by certain laws and privileges. Christians can use these things rightly and with a good conscience, just like all other political ordinances that are not at odds with the Word of God.

So far we have spoken about that part of the duty of Christians, by which they ought to keep themselves unsullied by participation in persecution of the Gospel, Christ, and His members, and from sin against the Holy Spirit in this war that is readied against us, and in the entire carrying out of the proscription of the Gospel and Christ along with our enemies, the apostates, whether they are to be done knowingly or unaware.

We now come to the second part of the duty of pious men, about which God has instructed us in Proverbs 24, saying, "Rescue those who are being led to death and do not refrain from freeing those who are being dragged to destruction. If you say, 'We did not have the strength to do so," He who is the inspector of the heart, He knows. Nothing can deceive the Preserver of your soul, and He will render to a man according to his works.

This discourse now warns Christians of two things: First, that it is not enough not to strive along with the impious against us, but that one ought also to be of aid to us, lest we be overwhelmed unjustly. And so, although the followers of Saul themselves did not lift their hands against the priests of Nob, nor did they consent to their murder, nonetheless, they were not innocent of the guilt of the murder that was committed, because they did not aid the innocent and defend them.

In the second place, this discourse warns Christians that those reasons to desert us which they are now inventing for themselves are not at all satisfying to God, that He should not hold them guilty of our blood and the blood of Christ, for whose sake we are suffering this persecution.

But these excuses are various. Some invent some excuses; others, others: that they are not able to decide because their superiors are making our rebellion, not our religion, an excuse for war; or that they lack the strength or the right to aid us against superiors, etc. God knows the emptiness of these reasons and whatever others they are able to think up now, and He proves in the consciences of individuals that they are not able to fool God, but will pay Him the penalties for this abandonment. Therefore this doctrine is an exposition of the fifth commandment, which makes guilty of murder not only those who take away life unjustly, but also those who do not rescue, as much as they can, either their own or others' lives from unjust violence.

If we are true members of Christ and members of one body joined together in Christ and made alive by His one Spirit, then truly there will also appear what the Apostle affirms about this body of Christ: When, he says, one member suffers, all the members suffer with it, and they are themselves distressed for each other, and bring each other mutual help.

Therefore those who have felt this distress, and do not immediately use their resources for the relief of the other, ailing members, are themselves either not members of the body of Christ, or are dead, or something less than half dead. For in a living body, it is impossible for living members not to be affected in turn, and for each one not to seek help, in its own place and manner, and bring aid to the other affected fellow members.

This is what this city [Magdeburg] deserves from the rest of the body of nearly the whole Christian Empire: not only should it not to be cast off, but it also can scarcely be abandoned without a great disaster for the body of the Empire. This city alone has published books exposing Interimistic and Adiaphoristic tricks. Without these warnings even the elect could have been led into error. Almost alone this city has resisted the schemes and attempts of the enemy, by which they strive to restore popery and destroy the liberty of our country, to the point that whatever of the pristine purity in the ministry is left outside our city, and what is left of liberty in the republic (plainly very little), God seems to have lavished throughout this city of His which He has chosen as his chaste virgin. And this virgin herself is spending her life and all she has not so much to preserve her own chastity and liberty as that of others. What sort of fairness will it be if others enjoy the benefits of this city, but are unwilling to take any share in her danger and inconvenience – especially in such a cause pertaining to the glory of God and the prosperity of the whole Church?

Here let them remember the most severe judgment of God, about which there is a severe and frightening story for those who desert the pious in Judges 5: When the two weakest tribes of Israel, Zebulun and Naphtali had risked their lives for the worship of God and the rest of the people against Jabin king of Canaan who was holding rule and exercising tyranny over the people of God, and the other more powerful tribes had rested, perhaps to await the outcome of this tragedy, in order that if the other army of enemies was victorious, they might be in less danger; while if God gave a happy outcome to their scanty and weak tribesmen, they themselves might enjoy the victory at the same time, without any labor or peril of their own, and when their brothers' blood had been shed and many of them certainly dead (just as is happening at this time), there God, not tolerating this great unfairness (not to say anything worse) ordered the deserter tribes to be cursed through His Angel, for He said, "They did not come to the aid of their Lord." He complains that, not men, but He himself was abandoned by His own.

But duties of this sort to which other pious persons are obliged to for the assistance of this city according to the saying of Solomon, are the following: First is intercession according to that verse of James 5, "Pray for each other."

We do not doubt the efficacy of those prayers, which in such a business of Christ Himself and His Church are being made by the consensus of true faith of all the members. They have divine power to change the outcome beyond the plans or strength of men, and have hitherto suppressed the raving of Satan, lest he immediately snuff out the remnants of the true ministry and true Church in our Germany.

The second duty is supplication with our superiors. If this were done with that unity of the majority of the States and of the pious which it ought to be, and with that confession of their own faith

and indication of duty in doing what is needed to defend the innocent for the common Gospel of Christ and for the sake of the whole
Church, then there is no doubt but that they would somewhat sway
the frenzied minds of the great princes to moderation, or restrain
them. If this seems hard to anyone[40], let him think, I pray, of that
passage of John where, just as Christ says that he laid down his life
for us, that is, to redeem us, so he orders us also to lay down our lives
for our brothers (John 3). Nor are our people here doing anything
else than bringing their own lives and all they have into the breach
for their brothers, just as much as for themselves. And some men
clearly acknowledge this kindness of ours toward them, that by the
defense of this city, those outside it are themselves kept safe against
extreme tyranny.

But indeed our very beseigers owe a great part of their own peace
and fortune to the few men who are still standing with us in true
piety and liberty. When these men are subdued, will not they, rather
than we, quickly feel the eagle's talons in their own feathers?

The third part of the duty of Christians arises from the previous
one. For when supplication has been made in vain, and the proper
confession has also been made, and the protestation of the duty of
preserving the innocent against unjust persecution, then the only
thing left for them to do is to put forth the same effort at preserving
Christ as the enemies are making at destroying Christ. Those who
are able also owe us that faithfulness which Jonathan and Hushai
showed to David when he was suffering injustices from King Saul
and from his son Absalom (1 Samuel 20, 2 Samuel 17). And indeed
they have helped us and the whole church not a little by their timely
forewarnings and the exceedingly sly plans of their Achithophels.

Last, to say something fuller for the duty which we have for the
glory of God and the salvation of all men: Think now, we ask you,
all you churches, and especially you rulers of them, who do not want
to betray and crucify the Christ you have acknowledged – think
how piously this is being done by you, that by your separation you
are deserting not only us, your brothers in Christ and members of
the same body of Christ, but also true piety and the Lord Christ
Himself, so long as you do not plainly oppose yourselves to the

---

40 Amsdorff uses a Greek expression, *"skleros houtos ho logos"*.

popish, Interimistic, and Adiaphoristic wolves, out of fear that you may suffer something serious.

You do not think that this struggle concerns you, and therefore, for the sake of your peace and pleasures, you watch it idly. Or is the damage that has happened – or rather, that is presently going on – not yet able to admonish you how prettily you have shown your wisdom, partly by lying low during the peril of your brothers, as though these matters did not pertain to you at all; and partly even by aiding the impious to inflict this calamity? At least you are prudent – or at least, after you have been stricken once, you allow yourselves to be warned about your duty by the outcome, which is how fools are usually educated.

Thus all the pious now ought to be affected in this common distinction of circumstances, just as if the members of their own bodies were being chopped off, or as if demons of hell were standing over them even now, about to snatch their souls away to eternal destruction – which, to be sure, will happen, so long as the true religion is snatched away from them by so many different sorts of tricks and violence.

Nor is there any reason why we should want to be broken in our spirits and despair so quickly on account of middling setbacks. For among Christians especially there ought to be true bravery of this sort, and it especially behooves them not to despair of God's deliverance even in the greatest straits. For we know that He is especially accustomed to bring his Church down to the depths, so that He may plan to bring her back up from there (1 Samuel 2). Affliction usually begins from the house of the Lord and ends at last upon the impious (1 Peter 4). We do not know the limit to these things, how far God will permit the impious to rave so against us. For the most part He delivers marvelously when things have been brought to the pitch of desperation and are plainly lost, as He delivered Jerusalem by a marvelous outcome when all the neighboring places had already been overturned (2 Kings 19); as He delivered Bethulia in its last desperation (Judith 7); and likewise Samaria (2 Kings 7); and the whole people, when He led them out of Egypt (Exodus, Joshua, Judges). Let us not, therefore, despair of the omnipotence of our God, nor let us imagine that His strength has been diminished by our weakness, or His arm made short. This cowardice of ours is a great crime.

Gentile men, who knew nothing certain about God, or about the immortality of the soul and eternal life, often submitted to death far more bravely on account of political causes, than we Christians – ah, shame! – do for the true religion of Christ. Oh what delicate Martyrs we are, not to say Epicurean bellies.[41]

Therefore let each of us do his duty with a brave heart in this most holy resolution to preserve the true religion – teachers by teaching, magistrates by bearing the sword, subjects by promptly obeying their governors when they command pious acts. For this is most certain, that we hold the true religion, and that we can do nothing more holy than to labor to conserve it, and thereby bring our lives and property into extreme danger – but each in his own place and rank, without confusion. For the preservation of true piety also especially magnifies the glory of God, and most of all preserves the salvation of one's neighbor, so that we can do nothing more pleasing to God in any situation, or anything more useful to our neighbor, than promoting and preserving true piety.

And here, let us diligently fix in our minds that opinion worthy of Christ, though said by a Pagan, and confirmed in various places throughout the Holy Scriptures, and let us meditate on it rightly: "Death is the end of life," said he, "for all men, even if you should wish to preserve yourself shut up in the most heavily fortified citadel." (Demosthenes)

Superior men of upright character ought also to undertake upright actions; ought set a good hope before them; and to bear bravely whatever God gives. Plainly we also ought to be subject to God, and to do with the utmost diligence whatever He orders, and leave the outcome to Him. But we have a sure promise that our labor that is undertaken according to His word will not be in vain, but will bear some fruit. Indeed, it is certain that Christ is with the Church, and that He will defend Her to the end even against all the gates of hell.

As for us individually, it is hitherto unsure whether we will escape from the present dangers of this life. For we ought each individually to be conformed to the son of God in this world, and pass through

---

41 Amsdorff means that Christians are devoted to pleasure rather than to God. Epicurus held that pleasure was the *summum bonum*.

various afflictions and at last through death itself into eternal life. But the promise to us is most certain, that whether we live or die, we are the Lord's (Romans 14), and that the light and momentary afflictions of this present life are increasing for us the weight of eternal glory beyond measure (2 Corinthians 4). Let us therefore do those things which are taught us by God, by retaining true piety, each of us in his own station with the utmost diligence, being certain that we have not been brought forth for this wretched and terribly brief life, but that we are hastening through this life to another, like travelers along some road. Let us be sure that we will doubtless be most blessed in that other life, though here we have suffered every evil for the sake of the Lord's name, and have been afflicted with every injury. For we will receive a hundred-fold, and will possess eternal life with Christ the Lord and all His blessed ones.

All that remains is for us all equally to beseech the God and Father of our Lord Jesus Christ that He may save us in the true confession of His son, and in all the proper duties which compel our confession; and that He may not allow us to be led away from these duties either by security, or timidity or wisdom, or conquered by the other enticements of this world. Thus may our Heavenly Father rule the outcomes of these dangers for all of us, lest the Antichrist with his father the Devil be able to triumph against Christ, and the people of the Antichrist be able to reproach the people of Christ, saying, "Where is their God? Where is their Gospel?" Come, therefore, Lord Jesus, come. Redeem us for the glory of Your name. He says, "I am even coming, and I am coming quickly (Revelation 22). For I will not give My glory to another (Isaiah 42), lest the gates of the world or of hell prevail against My Church (Matthew 16). Heaven and earth will pass away, but My words will not pass away (Luke 22). Praise be to Christ our eternal king. He lives and we shall live. We shall be glorified with Him, if indeed we also suffer with Him (Romans 8), and die for His sake all day long (Psalm 43). Amen.

Nicholas Amsdorff
Signed with his own hand
Nicholas Gallus, pastor at St. Udalric.
Lucas Rosenthal, at St. John.
Johann Stengel, at St. James.

Henning Freden, at St. Catharine.
Ambrose Hitfeld, at St. Peter.
Johann Baumgarten, at St. Spiritus.
Joachim Wolterstorp in the southern citadel.
Heinrich Gercken in our city.

The individual pastors and the other ministers signed by name with their own hands.

(Amsdorff adds this postscript. It is a eulogy for Stephanus Tucher, a pastor who apparently died during the siege of Magdeburg.)

On April 13, there departed from this life in the true confession of faith and in the invocation of the son of God, by a most peaceful death, M. Stephanus Tucher, our very faithful colleague in the Gospel of Christ at St. Udalric. The loss of him is felt most keenly among us. He had exceeding great erudition, skill in judgment, enthusiasm for true piety, and zeal that burned more than that of other men. His mind knew nothing of that Epicurean torpor by which many now suppose that these present struggles of religion are either of no importance, or do not concern them. And these qualities in him were sufficiently observed and proved both publicly and privately by many testimonies. Therefore, when we had come to see him struggling with his illness, some of us heard him condemn the Interimistic and Adiaphoristic tricks with great firmness and indignation of spirit, both at other times and especially a few days before his death – just as he also condemned them much earlier in his public writing which he prefixed to the commentary on Isaiah 53 by that man of God Dr. Martin Luther; and likewise to the discourse of Luther that he edited. Furthermore, they heard him urge us also to perseverance in this our confession against the spread of that Pharisaical leaven; and they heard him say many things pertaining to this matter with the utmost seriousness, which will perhaps be brought forth in their own place by others. But among other things, he ordered, when this book of ours was given to him to be published, that if we wished, we should add his own name also here, and that we should testify to the Church that he had died in the confession of the same opinion which this book contains.

And so, in order that we may be pious men and fulfill the request of a pious man, we have gladly added this note about his judgment, because we reckon that it will be of no small profit to the rest of the Church, for the strengthening of its judgment and for the glory of Christ. Even as he was dying he called upon the judgment of God, and was not disappointed in that invocation, so that he did not see or taste death, according to the word of Christ. This is the great testimony of a good conscience, and of the truth.

PSALM 93

The Lord reigns, He is clothed with glory.
The Lord has clothed himself and girded himself with strength.
He has even established the world, which shall not be moved.
Your throne is prepared from of old. You are from eternity.
The floods have lifted up, O Lord. The floods have lifted up their voice.
The floods have lifted up their waves, by the voice of many waters.
The lifting up of the sea is marvelous. The Lord is marvelous on the deep:
Your testimonies have been made very trustworthy:
Lord, your holiness adorns your house for all length of days.

[So ends the Magdeburg Confession]

HISTORICAL POSTSCRIPT

The siege lasted for over a year. About 4000 of Charles' forces were killed and 468 Magdeburgers lost their lives. The siege ended on November 4, 1551 with favorable terms for the Magdeburgers.

Maurice, now Elector of Saxony, grew tired of being called a "traitor" for switching to Charles' side for personal gain and private revenge. He was also unhappy that Charles was trying to re-impose Roman Catholicism upon all of Germany and beyond. Finally, he was bothered that his father-in-law, Phillip of Hess, who led the *Schmalkaldic League*, was still imprisoned four years after the battle of Muhlberg even though Charles had assured Maurice of his liberty.

Maurice again switched sides, thus precipitating the end of the siege. The *Interim*, requiring restoration of Roman Catholic sacraments, ceremonies, doctrines and rule would not be imposed upon the Magdeburgers.

Prior to and during the siege, the Magdeburg pastors and other Christians were busy writing. Not only did they produce what is now known as the *Magdeburg Confession*, but 228 known pamphlets were written, printed by the thousands, and distributed throughout Germany and to other nations during the siege.

The *Magdeburg Confession* and the stand these men took is known to have impacted John Knox, who led the Reformation in Scotland, and Theodore Beza, who was John Calvin's successor. Both of these men would build upon what was written and established there regarding the doctrine of the lesser magistrate.

If not for the actions of the Magdeburgers, the entire Reformation itself might very well have been a blip on the radar screen of history. Charles had intended to re-Romanize all of the Empire. However, the actions of these reformers clearly led to two very important councils and subsequent treaties.

After the siege ended, Maurice of Saxony, along with other German Princes attacked Charles and drove him out of Germany and into Italy. Charles V, tired of civil war, granted religious freedom to the Reformers at the *Peace of Passau* in August of 1552, just nine months after the siege of Magdeburg had ended.

The *Peace of Passau* granted peace only until another Imperial Diet could be held. The Diet was held in Augsburg in 1555. The result was the *Peace of Augsburg* (Sept. 25, 1555) which declared − *cuius regio, eius religio* ("whosoever region, his religion").

Greatest of all, the siege of Magdeburg produced the *Magdeburg Confession*, which is the earliest known historical document to lay out in a doctrinal format the *lesser magistrate doctrine*.

Further Reading about the Magdeburg Confession:

The Chancery of God – Magdeburg 1546-1551
Nathan Rein
St. Andrews Studies in Reformation History
Ashgate Publishing Limited 2008
First in-depth history written in English on the events surrounding the Magdeburg Confession

Theology of Revolution: Magdeburg, 1550-1551
Introduction: The Duty of Lesser Magistrates
Oliver K. Olson
The Sixteenth Century Journal Vol. 3, No. 1 (Apr., 1972), pp. 56-79
Published by: The Sixteenth Century Journal
Stable URL: http://www.jstor.org/stable/2539904

Tyranny and Resistance
The Magdeburg Confession and the Lutheran Tradition
David Mark Whitford
Concordia Publishing House 2001

Website: **LesserMagistrate.com**

Further Writings
Of Other Reformers
On The Lesser Magistrate Doctrine

The Appellation – 1558
John Knox
Selected Writings of John Knox
Kevin Reed, editor
Presbyterian Heritage Publishing, 1995

How Superior Powers Ought to be Obeyed by Their Subjects and Wherein They May Lawfully By God's Word be Disobeyed and Resisted – 1558
Christopher Goodman
Kessinger.net

On the Rights of Magistrates – 1574
Theodore Beza
http://constitution.org/cmt/beza/magistrates.htm

Made in the USA
Lexington, KY
06 March 2013